What People Are Saying About Investing for Cowards...

"Implementing the strategies in Fred Siegel's book will allow you to make big money in the stock market and still sleep at night. It should be read by investment professionals and novices alike."
> —Somers White, CMC, CSP, CPAE, president of The Somers White Company, Inc.

"Even during downturns in the market, Fred has minimized losses and we're still well ahead of where we started. We certainly will use the book to familiarize our grown children with Fred's concepts of conservative growth investments."
> —Rollie and Sondra Farris, clients

"*Investing for Cowards* shows how to put your money in solid companies—so-called 'Chicken Stocks'—that pay dividends and steadily grow earnings...And guess what? You'll prosper."
> —Jason Kelly, author of *The Neatest Little Guide to Stock Market Investing*

"Fred is a very stable, comforting presence. He has the long-range view in mind. This fits our philosophy. He's protecting our capital with growth. We want to generate 10% net return after all costs. He's done that or better."
> —Milan and Shirley Michalec, clients

"*Investing for Cowards* provides a seasoned view of investing. An investor who follows the framework set forth by Mr. Siegel should do very well in the stock market over the long-term and be able to sleep at night!"
> —Eric J. Aafedt, president, InvestmentHouse.com

"Fred is very professional, a step above, head of the class, in my opinion. I told my wife to just give the money to Fred and don't worry about it. That's how satisfied I am."
　　　—Barry Landry, client

"*Investing for Cowards* is a sound and effective long-term investment strategy for the conservative investor who might otherwise invest in bonds, or those investors who were "toasted" in the recent unwinding of the NASDAQ, technology-sector stocks and the dot-com mania."
　　　—Howard Blum, publisher, *Daily Economic
　　　Insights* newsletter; EconoNews.net

"We've listened to a lot of investment advisors. Fred is unique. We have a real relationship."
　　　—Mike and Nell Rodriguez, clients

"Fred Siegel's simple concepts and understandable, clear guidelines for choosing investments will help even those people who are terrified of investing. The strategies you learn will make sense and you'll actually feel comfortable entering this strange new world of investments, This is one book you should not procrastinate in reading."
　　　—Rita Emmett, author of *The Procrastinator's
　　　Handbook: Mastering the Art of Doing It Now*

"A gentle, friendly, and useful introduction to the stock market that is refreshingly humorous."
　　　—Greg Terry, publisher/editor,
　　　Wall Street Harvest

INVESTING
for Cowards

INVESTING
for Cowards

PROVEN stock strategies for anyone afraid of the market

FRED SIEGEL

Grammaton Press
New Orleans

Grammaton Press
601 Poydras Street, Suite 2650
New Orleans, LA 70130
(504) 566-3900
books@grammatonpress.com

Investing for Cowards:Proven stock strategies for
anyone afraid of the market / Fred Siegel

ISBN 0-9679366-6-7
Library of Congress Number 00-106036
10 9 8 7 6 5 4 3 2 1

Printed in Korea

Dedicated to
my wife, Elaine, the love of my life;
my mother, Sarah, the best around;
my father, Myron, who would have been proud;
and the people of metro New Orleans—
for your loyal support.

Contents

ACKNOWLEDGMENTS

In the early seventeenth century, Francis Bacon noted, "Reading maketh a full man, conference a ready man, and writing an exact man." I've learned the truth of those words in working on this book. I've also learned how important the people that surround you can be in helping to get the job done. I'm indebted to many who aided in numerous ways and were much more "exact" than me.

My partner, Wayne Traina, used his time and expertise in critiquing the raw manuscript. He also offered many helpful suggestions on the first typeset version of the book and, at times, worked more than usual in managing our business, allowing me extra time to spend on writing.

My assistant, Paula McGehee, and her administrative assistant, Katrice Harris, kept office operations in tip-top shape, freeing my mind for the prose you are holding.

Robin Bracken, Director of Administration for The Siegel Group International, worked diligently on the many details needed in publishing my book. Her hard work and suggestions were valuable to the finished product as well as the marketing effort.

Rick and Carolynn Crandall of Select Press provided excellent guidance, editing and page layout, making the book much more readable than it would otherwise have been. Rick's constant "nagging" was always appreciated and helped to get the manuscript finished in a reasonable time frame.

My publicists, Willie and Robyn Spizman of The Spizman Agency in Atlanta, have been great in directing the publicity effort.

My hat is also off to George Foster, the best dust jacket designer in the industry.

Of course, many people played a role in helping me to be in a position to write this book in the first place. Opportunities presented by well-timed phone calls have been instrumental in moving me toward this end.

A call by Stu Barnes more years ago than I care to admit got me into the investment business.

A call by Eric Paulsen inviting me to come "on set" at WWL-TV, to explain how to become financially independent, began a long-term relationship with the station and its viewers, a relationship that continues to this day. Regarding that, I would be remiss if I failed to thank former WWL-TV News Director, Joe Duke, for his support, guidance, and foresight in feeling his viewers would be interested in financial news. He was right! Present News Director Sandy Breeland and Station Manager Jimmie Phillips have continued in that forward-thinking vein and have been rewarded with top ratings.

Speaking of the media, I want to recognize the management team at WWL radio, and especially Diane Newman, for the chance to communicate daily to their listening audience and go in-depth every Saturday for a fun filled—at least for me—two-hour talk show. I also want to acknowledge Bob Christopher, formerly with WWL, for his encouragement and training in my "early days" at the station.

A call from Rene Lorio, President of Pan American Financial Advisors, and a subsequent meeting with Frank Purvis, Chairman Emeritus of Pan American Life; John Roberts, Chairman of Pan American Life, and Jan Jobe, President and CEO of Pan American Life, paved the way for starting my own investment advisory company, The Siegel Group, Inc. I must also acknowledge the superb cooperation I've received from the Pan American Life Board of Directors. This is a group whose "handshake" you can rely upon, something rarely experienced in today's society.

I thank John Durante, Branch Manager of the New Orleans office of PAFA for using his expertise to make it all work.

Beth Paris, my assistant from 1985 until September

1, 1999, also deserves special thanks for her devotion, loyalty, and work ethic in the "early days," through those interesting and tumultuous times on Wall Street. She played an integral part in building my business, a fact I will always appreciate.

I also wish to thank Jim Pagliaro for the opportunity to be a broker at the old Bache Halsey Stewart Shields; Greg Phipps for introducing me to the "Chicken Stock" concept; Somers White for showing me the importance of relationships in business, then providing me with many; and Larry Wachtel, Chief Investment Strategist at Prudential Securities—and the smartest man on Wall Street, for being my "mentor from afar."

Finally, my heartfelt appreciation goes to that beautiful blonde who walked out of the darkness at a convention in the old Atlanta-Fulton County Stadium and into my life. We married seven months later on February 15, 1970, beginning a fantastic, exciting, and memory-filled journey that continues to this day. Her loving support has been the foundation for everything I've done. To Elaine, my best friend, I say: "The best is yet to come."

AFRAID OF INVESTING IN THE STOCK MARKET?
You're Not Alone

---

*It's easy to make money in the market. If stocks
go up, buy them.
If stocks don't go up, don't buy!*
—W.C. FIELDS

WHEN MANY THINK OF THE STOCK
market, they think of...
- investing risk...
- danger...
- losing money...
- hot stocks going up, then down...

Investing your money can be a scary idea. And it doesn't matter whether you're a retired couple with no way to earn more money, or a "macho" self-made man. When you could lose your assets, it's scary!

That's why I wrote this book—for those who feel afraid or worried about investing. In fact, it's good to be a "cowardly" investor as defined in these pages. It's possible for the careful "coward" to have investment profits *plus* peace of mind.

In my experience, about 90% of investors I talk to are afraid of the stock market. Even experienced investors or people with high-risk portfolios feel "cowardly."

It's actually smart to be afraid of things you can't control or don't understand. In this book, I'll explain what you need to know about the stock market to control your risk while you are reaping the benefits of stock ownership. I'll show you how to safely preserve what you have, how to handle nervous moments, and how to come out on top. But first, let's discuss why most Americans are understandably afraid of investing in the stock market.

WHY AMERICANS HAVE A PHOBIA ABOUT THE STOCK MARKET

Whether you're a widow living on a fixed income or an entrepreneur who achieved financial success through your own business, you're still influenced by the 1929 stock market crash. Most of us, or our parents or grandparents, were directly or indirectly influenced by the Great Depression of the 1930s which was signaled by the Crash of 1929. It's easy to recall pictures of long "bread lines" of out-of-work people.

The idea that the stock market can crash overnight and wipe out security and wealth is part of American culture. The fact that the market operates differently today doesn't change this deep-seated phobia.

Wariness about the stock market and things you don't understand *does* serve a good purpose. Young investors can act foolishly. When investors have never seen stocks crash, and have never experienced double-digit inflation *and* double-digit interest rates at the same time, they think it can never happen.

What you need to keep in mind is that it's one thing to be cautious because you know that stocks can go down precipitously, and another to avoid investing altogether because of fear of the past.

2,600,000 Shares Sold In The Final Hour In Record Decline MANY ACCOUNTS WIPED OUT

(Headline from Thursday, October 4, 1929, *New York Times*)

HOW THE MARKET HAS CHANGED SINCE 1929

Few of the protections against market manipulation that we enjoy today were in place in 1929. Moreover, there was no Securities and Exchange Commission to closely monitor the market. There was no Social Security System to provide minimum incomes. (And, despite current problems with Social Security, the government won't take benefits away from people.) There was no automatic insurance of $100,000 on *multiple* bank accounts. There was no 50% margin requirement.

In other words, the market was much more risky in 1929 than it is today, but many people's underlying fears are the same. I understand how that can be. After all, there was a smaller crash in 1987 and a high tech stock crash in 2000.

FEAR AND IGNORANCE REMAIN

In 1948, a Federal Reserve Board survey found that approximately 90% of adults opposed buying stocks. Respondents gave two main reasons for their reluctance: About half said stocks were an unsafe gamble, and about half said they lacked knowledge.

Today, the percentage of people with some investment in the stock market is well over 50%, particularly if you count those investing through mutual funds and pension plans. Even so, fears about risk and lack of knowledge are still major factors that keep many people out of the market or limit their participation.

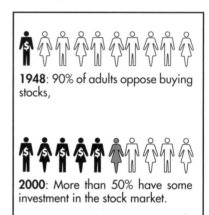

1948: 90% of adults oppose buying stocks,

2000: More than 50% have some investment in the stock market.

THE STOCK MARKET IS *NOT* A LOTTERY

Investors who lack knowledge continue to approach the market like a lottery—to them winning or losing is random. They behave as speculators and don't even realize it because they don't understand investments.

The reality is that there is still risk in the stock market, and people are often risking much more than they realize. We had a very favorable market for many years, from the late 1980s through early 2000. The market produced above-average returns over that period. Many speculative approaches succeeded because stocks did so well. Many young stock advisors have never known a stock market crash so, when it inevitably happens, they are unprepared.

YOU CAN PLAY IT SAFE

In this book, I'm going to cover a few approaches to the stock market that perform very well in strong markets. But, more important for the "coward" in all of us, they tend to preserve your capital in down markets. For instance, applying the principles of my "Chicken Stock" strategy in Chapter 3 will allow you to sleep at night. You won't make money in a down market, but you'll preserve more of your capital and be in a better position to make money when the market turns back up.

As you learn more about the stock market in the following pages, you will get more comfortable with the idea of investing. My basic concepts are easy to follow. As you apply my strategies to investing, you will understand what you are doing and why. This will further increase your comfort level.

> Why the term "Chicken Stocks"? Chicken Stocks are stocks that are good for people who are "chicken" or afraid of the stock market.

Let's take the case of "the Smiths" as an example...

A RETIRED COUPLE'S STORY

The Smiths are retired with grown children. Mr. Smith had worked for 35 years for a big company and Mrs. Smith had worked and raised the children. In addition to equity in their house and life insurance, they had several hundred thousand dollars in various IRAs and 401(k)s, plus Social Security. While they were comfortable, they felt they should be doing better. They were also worried about inflation and wanted to have an estate to leave to their children.

Most of their money was invested in *mutual funds* that had done well as the stock market went up in the 1990s. They were paying a lot of fees to the mutual funds, however, and didn't understand the differences between different funds' approaches. They came to me on a fact-finding mission. They wanted to get control of their money and reduce the number of separate accounts. They liked the idea of clear guidelines for choosing investments and immediately understood my approach. In the few years I've been working with them, their assets have almost doubled, creating more income as well.

Although I've changed the name and some of the details to protect confidentiality, the Smith's situation is a common one. They didn't know that there are *rules* for investing that they could understand and use.

MY STOCK MARKET PHILOSOPHY

I normally don't like to talk about myself. I like to think that my work for my clients speaks for me. My clients will tell you I've done well for them over a long period of time. Even so, early reviewers of this chapter asked me to add material about myself. And, since you may not know me, it's probably a good idea.

Over the course of 16 years, I worked and started six businesses, from construction clean-up to an overseas employment agency. These gave me very helpful insights into how businesses are run. I was able to sell them all for a profit. In 1981, I went to work for the New Orleans office of an international stockbrokerage firm.

There are two reasons I warn people about financial advisors who haven't been in the business since at least 1987. First, new brokers make mistakes and learn from them. I know I made a few and learned a lot in my early years. In fact, my favorite Chicken Stock strategy discussed in Chapter 3 is a modification of one I learned from Greg Phipps in my early days as a broker. Second, I was in the business during the 1987 crash. It's important that a broker *really* know that stocks go down as well as up.

After 18 years with major Wall Street firms, I now own my own business as a financial advisor, registered stockbroker, and portfolio manager. I spend my time managing about $80 million for individual clients and consulting with mutual funds, governments, and businesses around the world. (I once calculated that the total amount of assets I consult on is about $1.5 billion.) Generally, the individual clients I work with have from $500,000 to more than $2 million. I have associates in my firm who handle smaller accounts, following my direction. Companies, associations, and other groups also hire me to speak in order to help their people with investments. I hope this book will do the same thing for a broader audience.

As a personal aside, I also invest in the stock market myself and follow the principles in this book religiously. Regulators generally prefer that we not talk exact dollars. But I have about 95% of my investable assets in the stock market and have made enough to retire many times over. (I feel you should only do investment business with people who have substantial personal portfolios that they've made following their own advice.)

Enough about me. Now, back to our "program."

> We have a very strong relationship on the basis of comfort alone. The staff mirror Fred's excellent approach. And the results have been excellent, too.
> —Milan and Shirley Michalec, clients

Developing Your Philosophy

I have a very clear and straightforward investment philosophy that will be reflected throughout this book.

My goal is to help you feel comfortable protecting and increasing your net worth. I think you should be able to participate in the growth of the stock market and still sleep well at night. I want to show you how to clarify your own investment philosophy so that you can make your money work for you in ways you are comfortable with.

When you know more about the world around you, you have more control. When you bury your head in the sand, you invite trouble. When you depend on others to manage things you don't understand, you are giving up self-determination and others can take advantage of you.

You don't have to do a lot of work to understand my approach to investing. I will show you how simple the concepts really are. Then, if you wish, you can hire financial professionals to carry out the details as needed.

INVEST TO BUILD AND PROTECT YOUR WEALTH

Our economy is at a 100-year turning point. It's what I call a watershed event. New technology will affect us just as profoundly as many great inventions did a century ago (such as the automobile, the airplane, movies, and electric lights). Today, it's computers, biotech, the Internet, and so forth.

I'VE SLEPT WITH 5000 STOCKS!

When the late basketball star Wilt Chamberlain wrote his autobiography, he deliberately put in a paragraph about his having slept with 20,000 women in order to get attention. The thought alone is not only against my religious convictions but makes me tired! (I've been happily married to one woman since 1970.)

Nevertheless, I do want this book to be fun to read and thought the headline might wake you up! And—to make a serious point—**I've bought thousands of stocks and been able to sleep soundly at night.** You'll also be able to sleep at night with the investment strategies we'll be discussing in this book.

I'm going to state this up front: I have a bias for the strength of American business. While we are now inter-twined with the world economy, and there can be good investments around the globe, I stick with what I know—and trust—best. Other types of investments, like real estate, for example, can also be good in the right circum-stances. In this book, I'm going to focus on the American stock market.

YOU CAN WIN

With a sound strategy, you (the "little guy" as financial pundits refer to individual investors) can participate in the great growth that will occur over the next 100 years. As on Dorothy's journey along the yellow brick road to the land of Oz, there will be difficulties along the way. That's why you need to follow a *consistent* strategy. If you sin-cerely want to build and protect your wealth, you need to establish a good plan and stick with it.

This book will cover several ways to increase your in-vestment returns with improved safety. I'll describe my fa-vorite strategy in detail in Chapter 3. In a nutshell, my Chicken Stock strategy will show you how to buy stocks that have a "safety net" under them. While there is more than one strategy that can build your wealth, this one has been a winner for many years and I expect it to continue to be a winner for many more. It allows you to participate in the growth of the market while reducing much of the risk.

GETTING OVER YOUR FEAR OF STOCKS

Many times our fears are based on misunderstandings or misconceptions. I believe that, with the knowledge and understanding that you will gain here, you will be able to overcome your fears about the stock market.

False
Evidence
Appearing
Real

There are lots of reasons people fear the stock market:

- Some still think about *the* Crash of 1929. Some have friends who have lost money more recently.
- Stock scams do exist. Some "*boiler rooms*" call people at home to sell them the next great stock, bogus tax avoidance plan, or whatever—some people fall for the convincing stranger over the phone and lose their money. My rule for safety is that when you're called on the phone by a stranger about any investment, just say "No!"
- *Some* markets—like the commodities market—are very dangerous. Over 90% of investors usually lose money in commodities speculation. These are very bad odds. Don't confuse the commodities market with the stock market. In the legitimate stock market, *everyone can make money as they share in a growing economic pie.*

KNOWLEDGE BREEDS COMFORT

Most people lack knowledge about how the stock market works. For instance, a recent test found that most high school seniors answered only about half of the questions about personal finance and economics correctly. Past surveys have had similar results.

We tend to be wary of things we don't understand. Lewis Mandell, the University of Buffalo dean who conducted the survey, said, "There's so much choice it's bewildering. [But] if people are well informed, they can take advantage of the choices. If not, they become vulnerable." In other words, knowledge pays.

> We follow the market every day, but out of interest, not out of worry. Before we went with Fred, we rolled our 401(k) into the market and did badly. Even with the recent negative market, We're very pleased with Fred's results.
> — Mike & Nell Rodriguez, clients

WHY YOU SHOULD KNOW ABOUT THE STOCK MARKET

Given all the reasons to be afraid of the stock market, why not just leave it alone?

Because you are affected by stocks, whether you ignore them or not.

When you put money in the bank, government savings bonds, or guaranteed retirement plans (IRAs, KEOGHs), you are losing buying power to inflation unless your assets are going up. Inflation simply means that the cost of living is going up, so you need more money every year to buy the same things. Investments that don't provide you with higher income (or value) every year will hurt your economic standing. (You'll be poorer every year.)

Your banks, insurance companies, and pension funds invest your funds in the stock market. They know that the public stock market has outperformed most other investment options over the long term, as shown in the chart below. Typically, interest from banks and bonds is less than you could earn with a good stock market strategy. History has shown that the best way to maintain and increase your wealth over periods of 10 years or more, with liquidity and safety, is by investing in stocks. This makes it worth your while to become more knowledgeable about stocks.

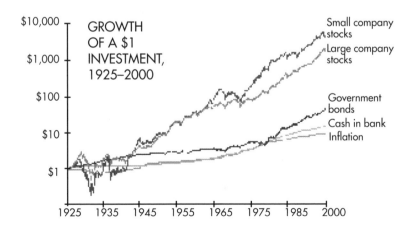

A dramatic example of how inflation can kill your buying power is shown in a series of ads that were run in major magazines like *Life* circa 1960. Take a look at the one on the opposite page. You wouldn't like to have to be living on that retirement income today!!

YOU DON'T HAVE TO DO IT ALONE

Learning more about stocks doesn't mean that you have to become an "ace" investor. You will benefit from simply becoming an informed consumer. The more you know, the better you'll be able to select stockbrokers, trustees, and others to manage your money or give you advice. When you know nothing, you are at their mercy.

When you develop your own investment philosophy, you can select people to help you who share your philosophy. That's what my clients do.

THE STOCK MARKET HELPS THE ECONOMY

Let's step back for a moment and talk about why the stock market exists and why it helps us all. Some people erroneously consider the market to be a giant gambling casino, but it actually serves an important economic function.

The stock market allows companies to raise money from the public. And it makes it possible for the public to invest in

OWN A PIECE OF AMERICA

Investing is a way to own a piece of corporate America. The money people invest helps companies buy the facilities and equipment they need to do business, and hopefully turn a creative idea into an exciting new enterprise. If the businesses people invest in make money, they receive a share of the profits. They own a piece of the company and are helping America grow.

How we retired in 15 years with $300 a month

"Look at us! We're retired and having the time of our lives. A fish story? It sure isn't! Let me tell you about it.

"I started thinking about retiring in 1950. Nancy thought I was silly. It all seemed so far away. 'And besides,' she said, 'it makes me feel old.' It didn't seem silly to me, though. We'd just spent the afternoon with Nancy's aunt and uncle. Uncle Will had turned 65 during the war, and, by 1945, his working days were over.

"Now life seemed to be standing still for them. They couldn't take even the short weekend trips that their friends could easily afford; they couldn't visit their children as often as they'd like.

"A pretty grim existence, I thought. But why? He'd had a good job. Then Nancy reminded me…they'd never planned ahead. During her uncle's working years, his paycheck was spent almost as soon as it arrived.

"Fortunately, they had put some money aside for a rainy day. But they hadn't planned ahead enough to make those retirement days sunny!

"Not for me, I decided. When it's time for me to retire, I want to be able to do the things we've always dreamed of doing instead of counting every penny.

"I showed Nancy an advertisement I'd seen in *Life* magazine a week or so before. It described their retirement income plan, telling how a man of 40 could retire in 15 years with a guaranteed income of $300 or more for life!

"Nancy agreed it was a great idea. The thought of retiring at 55 didn't make her feel old at all! So I filled out the coupon that day and sent it right off.

"A few days later the booklet describing the plans arrived. I picked the right one for us and signed up right away. Three months ago my first check arrived—right on time.

"Last month we moved down here to Florida, and we love it. Nancy looks great with her tan, and she's thrilled at the thought of keeping it all year long!

"My tan suits me fine, but I'm really hooked on the fish. Whether I catch one a day or ten (or none), I'm having the time of my life, because we saved for a sunny day with the Plan."

Send for free booklet

This story is typical. Assuming you start early enough, you can plan to have an income of from $50 to $300 a month or more—beginning at age 55, 60, 65, or older. Send the coupon and receive by mail, without charge or obligation, a booklet that tells about the Plans. Similar plans are available for women—and for Employee Pension Programs. Send for your free copy now. In 15 years you'll be glad you did!

TEXT OF AN ACTUAL ADVERTISEMENT CIRCA 1960

companies they believe will grow and become more valuable. This lets average people "own a piece of America" and receive dividends and increases in stock prices.

The stock market is a way for companies to get funding. An IPO (*initial public offering*) is when stock in a private company is sold to the public for the first time. It's a way for the company to raise money to build the business. In return, they give investors shares of the business and its value (growth in value or dividends). New companies create jobs and more business, and they give the public the opportunity to participate in the future value the companies may create.

"OLD" STOCKS

Most stocks that are traded are "old" stocks. Stock in companies like IBM and General Motors have been offered to the public for a long time. Having a public market for old stocks performs two vital economic functions:

1 COMPANIES CAN USE THEIR STOCK INSTEAD OF CASH TO BUY OTHER COMPANIES OR REWARD VALUABLE EMPLOYEES. For instance, Cisco, which produces cables, switches, and other infrastructure that supports Internet communication, has grown by buying dozens of smaller companies with its stock. It now has one of the highest market values of any high tech stock.

2 THE PUBLIC MARKET FOR STOCKS LETS OUTSIDERS (LIKE YOU AND ME) BUY A SHARE OF THE COMPANY EARNINGS, AND PARTICIPATE IN ITS ECONOMIC GROWTH. Having a market where stocks can be bought and sold easily (a "liquid" market) allows insurance companies, pension funds, and other institutions to participate in economic growth with the money they manage (yours and mine).

So, if someone tells you the stock market is just for gamblers, you'll know better. When people act like gamblers with stocks, they generally are unsuccessful. But you won't make that mistake after reading the rest of this book.

> Your ultimate success or failure will depend on your ability to ignore the worries of the world long enough to allow your investments to succeed. It isn't the head, but the stomach that determines your fate.
>
> —Peter Lynch, *Beating the Street*

WHAT IS RISK?

Since most people think that the stock market is risky, let's talk about what risk really is. Understanding risk will help you realize that you can never avoid it altogether. What you *can* do is avoid some risk, manage some risk, and better understand the risks you *really* face.

There are actually many kinds of risk. If you keep $1000 in cash in your house, for one week, there are risks. There are the risks of losing it, of robbery, and of fire.

When you put your $1000 into a longer-term investment, there are other risks.

Inflation Kills

Inflation is often "low"—prices for goods and services are going up only 2–3% a year. It doesn't seem to hurt at all. But, there are good reasons why President Ronald Reagan said, "Inflation is as violent as a mugger, as frightening as an armed robber, and as deadly as a hit man." The big risk of inflation is that it reduces your purchasing power over time. Even with only 2–3% inflation, those dollars you save at home or in the bank are going down in purchasing power every day. For instance, at 3% inflation, after ten years $100,000 would be worth only $73,740 in purchasing power. And there are times when inflation has been well over 10% (double-digit inflation). To stay even, you need to have income and assets that are growing with the economy. You need to have a "piece of the action." That's what stocks and a few other investments provide.

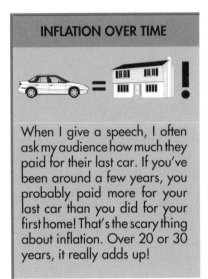

INFLATION OVER TIME

When I give a speech, I often ask my audience how much they paid for their last car. If you've been around a few years, you probably paid more for your last car than you did for your first home! That's the scary thing about inflation. Over 20 or 30 years, it really adds up!

Sometimes it may seem that I overstate the negative impact of inflation. I'm passionate about this topic because inflation is an insidious tax on all Americans. It not only erodes the purchasing power of your dollars, it pushes you into higher tax brackets.

Think about the ad on page 13 bragging about having $300 a month to live on— a comfortable amount in 1960. If you were in your prime earning years then, and planned your retirement according to those guidelines, you'd be living in poverty today! Thinking ahead 20–30 years is important if you expect to live a while, or want to leave an estate for your children and grandchildren.

The investments in the 1960's ad were considered very safe. They were guaranteed to give you a return, but they overlooked inflation.

Market Wobbles

Most stocks in the market may go down because of panics or declining economic conditions like the famous Crash of 1929. Market risks affect almost all investments, including bonds, real estate, and so forth. Being a long-term investor minimizes market risk because, over time, stocks have done very well. They've always gone back up after a decline.

Specific Disasters

A particular industry or company may have bad things happen to them (for example, a fire in the main shaft of a diamond mine company). This is also true of other investments. These risks are almost impossible to predict. To reduce these risks, you need to diversify your investments and hold stocks in different companies and industries.

Economic Fluctuations

When bad economic news hits, people feel less optimistic and more investors are selling than buying. (Since the stock market is like an auction, when there are few buyers who want to purchase a stock, the price usually will have to be lowered before someone is willing to buy.) Again, being a long-term investor protects you from this kind of up and down, cyclical risk.

> People think that investing is a risky undertaking. In fact, the bigger risk is run by those who cautiously stash all their funds away in bank accounts and other low-paying savings vehicles. They risk the certainty that their money will lose ground to inflation.
> —Caroline Donnelly, *Money* magazine

Interest Rate Dance

Bonds and fixed-income investments like CDs will go up and down with interest rates. For example, banks pay less interest when rates go down. And if you're holding a bond, its value goes down when interest rates go up. Unless you hold it to maturity, you can lose money when you sell a bond early. (See Chapter 6 for more details.)

Statistical Mumbo Jumbo

Academics and others have invented various measures of risk such as *alpha* and *beta* that reflect how risky a stock is compared to the average stock. They then use these invented measures of "risk" when talking about risk in the stock market. However, these risk measures may not relate to reality, like your risk of losing money. The charts here will give you an idea of why these types of artificial measures can be misleading.

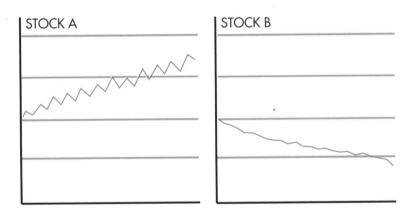

The first chart shows a very good stock. Stock A goes up consistently, with some ups and downs. Stock B is a loser. It goes down gradually all the time. Yet, Stock A could have a higher "measured" risk. Academics could rate it much riskier than Stock B because its price has more ups and downs! Common sense and statistics don't always go together.

YOUR ATTITUDES AND CONCERNS ABOUT INVESTING

On the next few pages there are some questions to help you understand your attitudes toward risk and investing, and some items about your finances. Some people are so uncomfortable about investing that they will be nervous even with a good investment strategy.

When I interview new clients, we first go through a checklist so that I can understand their situation and to help them clarify their investment goals. Sometimes we do this in person and sometimes we do it over the phone. The following are some of the general types of questions we might discuss.

YOUR PRACTICAL RISK ISSUES

These questions check how much money you have, need, and expect in the future. They also check whether you have time to establish long-term investments.

1. How soon will you need the money back that you invest?
   - ❏ in less than a year
   - ❏ 1–2 years
   - ❏ 3–5 years
   - ❏ 6–10 years
   - ❏ don't really need it

2. Is your present income sufficient for your daily needs?
   - ❏ no
   - ❏ yes

3. Do you need income now from your investments?
   - ❏ no
   - ❏ yes

4. If you're working now, do you have extra money to invest regularly?
   - ❏ no
   - ❏ yes

5. If you're happily retired, do you need to take money from your investments regularly?
   - ❏ no
   - ❏ yes

6. About how much do you have in liquid assets (cash or assets you can get your hands on in 30 days such as bank accounts, stocks, and so forth)? $ _____

7. Do you expect any windfalls in the next few years (such as an inheritance, sale of assets, and so on)? If yes, how much money, and when? $ _____   When? _____

8. Do you have any big, new expenses coming up (such as college costs for children)? If yes, how much will you need, and when?
   $ _____   When? _____

9. Do you have enough money for your retirement?
   ❏ no
   ❏ yes
   If yes, how much extra will you need? _____

YOUR FEELINGS OR ATTITUDES

These next questions are trying to determine how you feel about risk (your risk tolerance) in your investments.

10. How does the idea of making a 20% profit on an investment make you feel? ☹ 😕 😐 🙂 😊

11. How does the idea of losing 20% on an investment makes you feel? ☹ 😕 😐 🙂 😊

12. Which would you prefer:
   ❏ an investment that could either lose 30% or gain 150% over 10 years.
   ❏ an investment that could lose nothing or gain 50% over 10 years?

13. Seeing a $25 stock I owned go down $3 per share in a week would bother me this much: ☹ 😕 😐 🙂 😊

14. If the stock market fell by 25% this year, and your stocks with it. Would you:
   ❏ feel bad and consider selling some/all stocks.
   ❏ be concerned and continue to watch the market.
   ❏ not worry, because the market is likely to go up again in the next few years.

15. If I knew more about the stock market:
     ❑ I'd probably be more comfortable.
     ❑ I'd still be bothered by the ups and downs.

16. I often put off making financial decisions because I am afraid of making a mistake.
     ❑ no
     ❑ yes

17. I believe I should know something about my investments.
     ❑ no
     ❑ yes

18. My lack of knowledge about investments keeps me from becoming more involved in my own financial affairs.
     ❑ no
     ❑ yes

"Scoring" Yourself

The questions above are not based on scientific data. They are designed to give you some insight into your situation and feelings. (And to help me understand you if we were to work together.) The first nine questions answer whether you can afford to invest and what income you need now. If you don't need a quick return on your investment, or are more concerned about the future, or even your estate, you can reduce your risk by investing for the long term (more about this later).

The last nine questions (10–18) show how you *feel* about investing. If you simply can't stand thinking of your stocks going down occasionally, and are afraid even if you know you don't need to be, then you can keep your money where your principal is guaranteed, such as in government notes. I'll cover the best ways to do this in a later chapter, although growth of your money will be limited.

OVERVIEW OF THIS BOOK

Chapter 2 is a short chapter that goes over some **basic stock market jargon** and other information, such as how to read a stock listing and chart.

As mentioned already, Chapter 3 covers my favorite investment strategy using **"Chicken Stocks."** These are stocks that provide stability and growth for "cowards"—or anyone who is cautious (or chicken) of the stock market. These successful companies provide higher income every year, with underlying growth in value. I could have saved the best for last, but I wanted to jump right in for you to see some of the benefits of investing in stocks for the long run.

Chapter 4 covers **mutual funds**. Even though mutual funds are the favorite investment of most smaller investors, and they have their advantages, I don't recommend them for most people. Mutual funds have several important limitations that are seldom discussed.

Chapter 5 covers **unit trusts**. In several different forms, they are a type of investment that is a variation of mutual funds that few stock brokers or investors use or understand. For the serious investor, they overcome many of the limitations of mutual funds and provide greater control of investments while allowing diversification.

Chapter 6 covers **bonds**. For the conservative investor who needs income *now*, bonds can be a way of preserving your principal. Using a technique called "laddering" helps you stabilize the income and principal. Bonds, however, have large risks if they are sold before maturity. And most expose you to inflation risk, which is a big disadvantage.

Chapter 7, "The Great American Premium Machine," covers an often-overlooked type of bond—**convertible bonds**. These bonds provide some of the stability of bonds with some of the upside of stocks. I also show you how to get extra income from these bonds.

Chapter 8, "So You Want a Guarantee," covers a much misunderstood, and often controversial, investment—

annuities. These are investments sold by insurance companies that give you a guaranteed return. Unfortunately, the return is usually after you're dead! Nevertheless, annuities are adding some new features that are ideal for the ultra coward. The latest generation guarantees you a return *during your lifetime*, while allowing you to be in the stock market.

Chapter 9 covers **stockbrokers and other financial consultants**. These experts *may* provide good value for you. Unfortunately, they can also be the *biggest risk* to your financial health. Too many of them do not have good track records, do not have enough experience, and are interested more in trading stocks (they love those commissions!) than in helping you come out ahead.

In Chapter 10, I'll give you a tour of the world of **online investing**. This is an exciting and growing area for people who want to manage their own money. Unfortunately, it is also a bit like the Wild West without sheriffs. Some of the people providing advice online are doing a good job, but many of them are touting investments and scams designed to transfer your money into their pockets. Every month, new examples of scams involving online investing are uncovered. Be careful and know who you are dealing with here.

Chapter 11 covers **market crashes**. The market has been consistently positive over long periods of time. But there can still be periods where it goes sideways or lower for months or even years. For instance, many high tech stocks crashed 50% or more in the year 2000, and some stocks or industries remain stagnant for years. This chapter discusses what to look out for and how to deal with the market during these negative periods. It also covers famous historical crashes.

Chapter 12 talks about **how you can put it all together** and move ahead as a successful investor. It discusses the psychology of investing, and the factors that separate winners from losers. It will help you decide what to do now.

SUMMARY

Stocks are nothing to fear if you use a sound strategy and apply it consistently. We've covered an overview of the market and book here. In the next chapter, I'll go over some basic concepts like price-earnings ratios, how to read stock tables, and investment jargon. If you're already familiar with these basic concepts, you may want to skip Chapter 2 and move right to Chapter 3, where we get into my Chicken Stock strategy.

2

JARGON, CHARTS, AND OTHER TECHNICALITIES

...this society hath a peculiar chant and jargon of their own, that no other mortal can understand..."
— JONATHAN SWIFT

IN THIS CHAPTER I'M GOING TO cover some basics like how to read a stock table and stock charts. If you already know the basics, feel free to skip to the next chapter. Terms are defined in the back of the book, but many people find financial terms intimidating, so I'll cover a few here.

JARGON: WHAT DOES IT ALL MEAN?

I can visualize you, the reader, backing away at terms like "principles of investment." Yes, it does sound intimidating. But, so does the terminology of any field you're not familiar with. Have you ever heard two wine aficionados speaking of "bouquet" and "bottle sickness," or two computer geeks talking of "ROM" and "BIOS," or two gardeners speaking of "thrip" and "air layering." It *is* intimidating, until you pick up the jargon.

In most fields, the concepts are simple, but we think they are complex when we don't understand the words. You don't need to know the terminology to enjoy a glass of wine, use a computer, or grow a garden. As you expand your knowledge, you expand your appreciation and enjoyment of the subject—and understanding of the jargon! It's the same with stock market lingo.

> Incomprehensible jargon is the hallmark of a profession.
> —Kingman Brewster, US Ambassador to Britain

> *Everyone would benefit from understanding something about the economy and the stock market.*

The economy and stock market affect your financial situation, whether you like it or not. It's a shame that these basics aren't taught in school. The more you know, the better off you are.

Investing is not "rocket science." The basics are very simple. The more you know, the more comfortable you'll be with your money. And, perhaps you can even pass on that knowledge—and your increased comfort—to your children or grandchildren. It's time we broke the historic American phobia about the stock market. The Crash of 1929 was a long time ago. It's a new world and, in many ways, a better one.

THE BASICS

As mentioned in Chapter 1, a stock is a small share of a business. If a company has 10 million shares and you own 100 shares (a *round lot*), you own .00001 ($1/100,000$) of the company. As a shareholder, you get to help select who will run the company by voting for people to be on the board of directors.

Earnings

The primary reason for owning a share of a business is so you can share in the profits. If a company with 10 million shares makes a $10 million dollar profit, then each share earns $1.00. The company may then use these profits to reinvest in the company for developing new products or building new factories. Reinvesting in the company generally increases the value of the company. A company may also distribute some of the profits to shareholders—this distribution is called *dividends*.

Dividends

Dividends are the money a company pays to shareholders. They are like interest on your money in the bank, except they are mailed directly to you or your brokerage account, unless you instruct them to use the dividends to buy more stock.

Some companies don't pay any dividends because they have projects they are confident will make them high returns on their money. If they can make 50% on the money they reinvest in the company, it will increase the value of the company (and the value of the stock you own). High earnings will push the price of your stock up, even if the company never pays dividends.

> *Dividends are what you can spend without selling your stock.*

Bonds

The same companies that issue stock to raise money can also issue *bonds.* Bonds are simple borrowings or debt. Companies borrow money by selling bonds. They then pay a predetermined interest rate and usually pay back the debt at a specific time. Unlike stocks, bonds are also issued by governments (for example, *Treasuries*) and non-profit agencies. Interest from many government bonds is tax free at either the state or federal level. With bonds, you do not own a piece of the company.

Bonds are worth a specific amount—usually $1000 each—if you hold them to "maturity" (the date they can be redeemed). If you sell before maturity, however, their value may be more or less than you paid (see Chapter 6 for a complete discussion of bonds).

HOW TO READ THE STOCK TABLES

In every daily newspaper there is a stock table that lists prices from the day before. Stock tables are simple, once you know how to read them. But you have to know a few bits of information. First, you have to know in which market the stock is bought and sold because there are separate listings for the New York Stock Exchange, the American Stock Exchange, NASDAQ (pronounced "naz dack"; North American Securities Dealers Automated Quotations), and some small regional exchanges. If you're not sure which exhange a stock is on, you can probably find it by checking the alphabetical listings of companies for each of the three major exchanges, or you can ask your broker. The most difficult things about reading the stock tables are the tiny print and recognizing the abbreviations for the names of the companies.

In the chart below, I'll go through some typical listings one part at a time. You'll see that each part is simple, once you know what it is saying. I'll read the listing with you, one column at a time, from left to right.

Here is an example of several stock listings as you might find them in the newspaper:

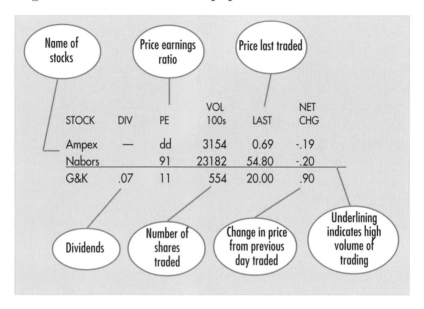

Stock names. In the table above, the first company is Ampex. That is the name of a company that makes audio components. Usually the stock names listed are abbreviations and you can figure most of them out (for example, Microsft = Microsoft, BarnNbl = Barnes and Noble). But sometimes the abbreviation doesn't have much relationship to the actual name and you need to check the list of stocks you own. Sometimes the stock tables also list the "ticker tape" symbol for your stocks. These are even briefer and harder to guess. These symbols are usually on your brokerage account statement or in a listing of stocks available at the library by alphabet (such as *Standard & Poor's* or *Value Line*), from your broker, or online at many Web sites. Once you know the abbreviations and ticker tape symbols of your stocks or mutual funds, write them down somewhere. You'll find them easy to remember after a while.

Dividends. The next column (DIV) indicates that Ampex pays no dividend.

Price earnings ratio. The next column (PE) stands for *price earnings ratio.* This is the price of the stock divided by the earnings of the company over the last year. This is a quick way of seeing how the company is valued. If the average stock sells at a PE ratio of 20, that means the price is 20 times more than earnings. If another stock sells at a PE ratio of 40, it means it is more popular so people are willing to pay more for each dollar of earnings. Often this is because they anticipate that earnings will go up soon. In the opposite case, when the PE ratio is lower than the market, say, 10 in this case, it means the stock is not as popular. Sometimes buyers are anticipating future problems.

AN EXAMPLE OF THE PRICE-EARNINGS RATIO

Here are two companies whose stocks are both valued at $100 a share. But one of them earns $4 per share a year, and the other $10 per share a year.

	ABC Toys	XYZ Computers
Cost per share	100	100
Earnings per share	4	10
PE ratio	25	10

For ABC Toys, the PE ratio is 25 (the price of the stock divided by the earnings); for XYZ Computers, the PE ratio is 10. Both stocks cost the same, so why wouldn't you just buy XYZ Computers? After all, it earns 2.5 times more. XYZ Computers *might* be a good investment. But if it's such a good investment, why aren't more people buying it? A low PE ratio acts as a warning to check a particular stock out in greater detail— it might be a great bargain or there might be negative factors associated with the company that are inhibiting other investors from buying the stock.

In the Ampex case, the "dd" in the PE column means that the stock lost money in the past year, so a ratio would not be a sensible number. Your stock tables will have some footnotes or other guides explaining abbreviations like these.

Number of shares traded. The next column (VOL 100s) is how many shares were traded, in hundreds. So in the Ampex case, 2550 times 100 equals 255,000. That's the number of shares that were traded the day before.

Last trading price. The next column (LAST) is the last trading price of the stock for that day, in this case, $2.81. That is the price at which the stock "closed."

Net change. The last column (NET CHG) is net change. If it is positive, it means the stock went up that much. If it is negative, it means the stock went down—in this case, 19 cents.

Underlining. Notice that the second stock listed is underlined. The underlining indicates a lot of trading activity. For the listings for the New York Stock Exchange and the American Stock Exchange, underlining indicates that at least 1% of the outstanding shares were traded. For the NASDAQ, underlining means that at least 2% of outstanding shares were traded. If there is a lot of trading in a stock, it usually means there is something happening. Check with your broker if you're interested.

Now that you can read a stock table, take a look at G&K (G&K Services) in the third row. This stock pays one 7-cent yearly dividend based on the current rate of payments (usually quarterly). It trades for 11 times earnings, and traded 55,400 shares. It last traded for $20, which was up 90 cents from the previous day.

THE NEW YORK STOCK EXCHANGE

The New York Stock Exchange generally deals with the largest stocks. Its stock listings usually contain the above information, plus the highs and lows for the last 12 months. Now that you know how to read the basic information, the following will be easy for you:

52-WEEK					VOL.		NET
HIGH	LOW	STOCK	DIV	PE	100s	LAST	CHNG
134.94	80.06	IBM	.80	26	142777	111.25	+2.94

This listing tells us that stock in IBM has varied between $134.94 at the high and $80.06 at the low for the last 12 months. It pays a dividend of 80 cents and has a PE ratio of 26. Yesterday, 14,277,700 shares were traded and the last sale was at $111.25, up $2.94 from the previous day.

The annual price range information is useful. It gives you a rough estimate of what price the shares could sell at in the future, and how close to the bottom or top the stock price currently is.

MUTUAL FUND LISTINGS

Mutual fund prices are listed by their sponsors' names. Sponsors often have multiple funds. For instance, in my local paper, there are listings for 36 funds managed by Scudder. One such listing follows.

	SALES LOAD	1-YEAR RETURN	NAV	1-DAY NET CHNG
Scudder				
Income S	NL	+.7	12.63	-.03

This is an income fund that trades at $12.63 (the value of its holdings, *net asset value;* NAV). It was down 3 cents on the day. The *sales load* indicates how much an investor is charged for each $100 purchased. A sales load of 5 would mean a 5% charge; "NL" stands for "no load," which means there is no sales charge. The one-year return represents the change in the value over the last year with all income and capital distributions reinvested.

BOND LISTINGS

Bond listings are seldom in your daily paper. Often they are listed only once a week or not at all. Investment publications like *The Wall Street Journal* and *Investors Business Daily* list them more often.

Bonds can be listed by exchanges, such as the New York Exchange, or by type, such as US Treasury Bills or US Zero Coupons.

Here's a sample bond listing:

52-WEEKS		NAME &	CURR	SALES	-WEEKLY-			NET
HIGH	LOW	COUPON	YLD	$1,000	HIGH	LOW	LAST	CHNG
110¼	97	IBM 7½ 13	6.9	297	109½	106⅝	109	+1

ZERO-COUPON BONDS

Most new bonds have a $1000 purchase price (value) and they pay a specific interest rate such as 7% yearly. Zero-coupon bonds don't pay regular interest. Instead, you buy them at a discount and they are redeemed for $1000 at a specific time in the future. The amount of the discount can be calculated as a specific interest rate. (See Chapter 6 for more information.)

"IBM 7½ 13" in the name and coupon column tells us that the IBM computer company issued bonds paying 7½% interest that mature (are paid off) in 2013. In the columns at the far left are the high and low prices for the last 12 months. In the last year, the price of this bond varied from $970 to $1102.50. (Notice that, in bond tables, the prices need to be multiplied by 10.) Moving to the right, the current yield (rate of interest based on current price) is 6.9% and 297 bonds (valued at $1000 each) were traded. In the last week, the price varied from $1066.25 to $1095. The last sale was for $1090 (109), a price that was up $10 (+1) from the day before.

STOCK CHARTS

Stock charts are a way of summarizing a lot of information about a stock in visual form. Sometimes pictures are easier to understand than words or numbers. Most charts condense a lot of information. Stock charts are designed and owned by different companies, so they will highlight different types of information. Charts can be plotted over days, months, years, or even hours.

IT'S CORNY YOLK TIME

TODAY'S STOCK MARKET REPORT

Cluck, cluck!

- Paper was stationary.
- Fluorescent tubing was dimmed in light trading.
- Knives were up sharply.
- Pencils lost a few points.
- Hiking equipment was trailing.
- Elevators rose, while escalators continued their slow decline.
- Weights were up in heavy trading.
- Light switches were off.
- Diapers remained unchanged.
- Shipping lines stayed at an even keel.
- The market for raisins dried up.
- Coca Cola fizzled.
- Caterpillar stock inched up a bit.
- Sun peaked at midday.
- Scott Tissue touched a new bottom.

The chart on the next page has the years listed along the bottom. It also has the volume of trading for each month of the year with the scale at the bottom along the left.

The main "line" will be the stock price. Prices will be marked along the left or right side. In this case, stock prices are on the right and the scales for earnings and dividends are on the left. The price is indicated as a bar chart showing the high and low point for each month. Other lines on

ABBOTT LABORATORIES (ABT)

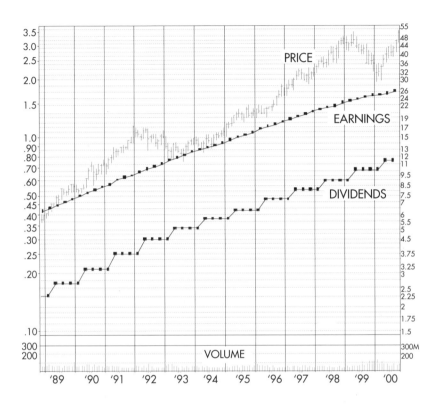

the same chart could include the dividend payments, earnings, and the comparison price of the *Dow Jones Industrials* (an average of 30 actively traded stocks of well-established, blue-chip companies that is designed to reflect the general state of US business). Each chart maker will have some other information on the chart, usually labeled clearly.

The good thing about charts is that they give you a quick idea of how the stock has acted over the longer term, along with its earnings and dividends. If the trend of all three is up, you know it has been a good performer. When the price varies decidedly from the other trends, something new may be happening that you want to find out about before making an investment decision.

SUMMARY

If you're comfortable with the information in this chapter, you can see that stocks are not so mysterious. You now probably know more about the stock market than 90% of the general public. In the next chapter, we'll roll up our sleeves and get into my favorite strategy for cowards...the Chicken Stock strategy.

3

CHICKEN STOCKS IN EVERY POT

*I'm a great believer in luck, and I find the harder
I work the more I have of it.*
—THOMAS JEFFERSON

LONG AGO, KING HENRI IV OF France declared, "I want there to be no peasant in my kingdom so poor that he is unable to have a chicken in his pot every Sunday." In the 1920s, Louisiana politician Huey Long promised people that, if they'd vote for him, he'd put a chicken in every pot. Herbert Hoover, in his 1928 campaign, promised Americans "two cars in every garage and a chicken in every pot." Because I'm from Huey Long territory and because this chapter is about my Chicken Stock strategy, I couldn't resist having a little fun with the play on words in the title. But I'm also serious. I want *everyone* to reap the benefits from Chicken Stocks.

There's an old saying on Wall Street that "bulls make money, bears make money, but hogs get slaughtered." That means that you can make money when stocks go up (a bullish market), and you can make money when stocks go down (a bearish market), but if you get greedy (hoggish) you're likely to lose.

In this chapter, I'm going to tell you about my favorite investment strategy for "cowards." To that bulls-bears-hogs saying, I'd like to add a phrase:

Chickens can make money, with little danger of getting slaughtered.

I use the term "chickens" to refer to people who are afraid of the stock market. Unlike many investors, chickens don't expect quick gains. They use my historically proven strategy to hold a key group of superior stocks that meet my strict

LET ME TELL YOU ABOUT THE BEARS AND THE BULLS

 A bear market is one in which stock prices are falling. A bull market is a rising market.

Common wisdom is that these terms come from the way bears and bulls attack—bears attack by swiping their paws downward and bulls toss their horns upward.

However, according to fool.com, the origin of bear market actually comes from "bearskin jobbers"—trappers in days of yore who would sell skins of bears they had not yet caught. This term then came to be used to describe "short sellers." (Short sellers borrow and sell shares of stocks they don't own with the expectation that their price will drop. They hope to buy them back at a lower price to replace the stock they borrowed.) Obviously, "bears" hope the market will go down.

During that same time period, having bulls and bears fight each other was a popular sport, and bulls came to be seen as the opposite of bears. Thus the bulls were those people who bought in the expectation that a stock price would go up.

criteria. They don't try to predict every up and down move of the stock market. They know that nobody is smart enough to do that over any period of time. Even if you're right about the market going up or down, it's almost impossible to tell exactly when it will move. Short-term movements of stock prices often have more to do with emotion than underlying stock values.

SHORT-TERM PRICES ARE RANDOM

The price of a stock is random and unpredictable over the short term. (And the short term can last a year or more!) But over the long term, a stock's price tends to keep up with its earnings and dividends.

Short-term movements of stocks are the most misleading aspect of the stock market. Every day you hear smart people on the news and in the paper "explain" why the market was up or down. The reasons given are logical—"fear of rising interest rates drove the market today," "weak earnings reports," "export trade figures," and so forth. I do this myself on radio and television.

Fortunately for us Chickens, in the long run, stock earnings and dividends always determine prices. Stocks of companies that earn more money become more valuable be-

WARREN BUFFET: THE WORLD'S BEST INVESTOR

In the early 1950s, Professor Graham of Columbia University was one of the country's most highly regarded stock analysts. Graham advised Warren Buffet not to invest his $10,000 then, when the Dow was at 250, but to wait until the Dow went down to 200. Buffet says, "If I'd followed Professor Graham's advice, I'd still have $10,000 today." (Stocks never again went as low as 200.) The point is that, if the smartest stock analyst can't predict the ups and downs of the market, what makes anyone think they can.

cause more people buy them. Under good management, higher earnings are eventually paid out in dividends or reinvested in the business to increase value.

BUY REAL COMPANIES, NOT PAPER

The secret of common-sense Chicken Stock investing is to remember that you are buying shares in *real* companies.

Too many people talk about the stock market or stocks as if they were real things in and of themselves. Too many investors (and their advisors) buy and sell

The ups and downs of stock prices that "experts" explain are usually statistically insignificant. That's a fancy way of saying that 100 points means nothing when the index is at 10,000. Also, explaining price movements after the fact is *not* the same as predicting them ahead of time!

stocks without thinking about what they actually represent. I said the following in the last chapter when explaining how the stock market contributes to the economy, but I want to restate it here a little differently:

> *Every share of stock represents a piece of a real company. The earnings (or potential earnings) of the underlying company are the major factor in giving a stock value.*

This point may be obvious to you, but many professional investors forget it. In this book, I talk about *stocks*. But before we get too far, I just want to emphasize that it is the *companies* we are buying. When you own a stock, you own a small piece of a company. If a company makes money, the stock will be worth something. If the company doesn't, it won't. (There are cases where a stock doesn't make money for years when the company is building the business—such as MCI Telephone or Amazon.com. But investors buy on the assumption that they *will* make money later. If the companies never produce profits, their stock prices go down.)

The most important thing a good company can do for its owners is make money. With this money, it can contribute to the community, it can advertise to attract more customers, it can invest in product development and customer service to make customers happy, and it can pay you a dividend representing your share of the extra earnings. This can be self-perpetuating.

When companies grow, their stock prices generally go up. Because great companies reinvest money in customer service and new products for customers, they will grow. They then make more money to invest in the business to grow even further, or pay higher dividends, or both.

Investing in a well-run company with a stable board of directors is certainly safer than depending on the politicians we elect to take care of us financially.
— Dottie and Barry Landry, clients

INVESTING IN A CHANGING STOCK MARKET

It turns out that the companies that fit my Chicken Stock strategy look "lucky." They do things right while others struggle. But this is because they also fit Thomas Jefferson's rule—they've worked hard to become great companies that produce needed goods and services. This is what gives them superior results year in and year out.

We know that the overall stock market has done very well for the last 100 years or so, especially if you invest for periods of five to ten years. So, what every investor wants to do is buy shares in great companies that will do at least as well as the overall market in good times and maintain more of their value during bad times. My Chicken Stock strategy allows you to do just that.

Danger + Opportunity = Change

The meaning of the Chinese ideograph for change contains two different symbols. The first means threat (or danger) and the second means opportunity. When you think about it, change brings both. And as the old song says, "The times, they are a'changin'." The truth of that lyric has become more and more obvious over the past couple of decades. The changes around us should have a major impact on how you view your money and investments now and in the future.

The biggest change is that we are living longer and better. In Chapter 1, I talked about inflation and how it can eat away the value of your assets. According to the US Census Bureau, a man used to retire at the age of 65 and die when he reached 72. That means he would, on average, need to have enough money to support himself for seven years, with life insurance coming to the aid of his wife. Now, however, the average man retires earlier and lives longer. That often translates to 20-plus years of retirement, and it's growing longer every day. Women continue to outlive men, so they need even more money, whether

As Will Rogers once said, "It's not the return *on* my investment that concerns me as much as the return *of* my investment."

from their own retirement funds or insurance.

BUYING INTO A BUSINESS

Surveys tell us that the majority of wealthy people got that way by owning their own business. You can do the same by buying pieces of great American businesses in the stock market. Of course, as we discussed in Chapter 1, when stocks are mentioned, there is a lot of fear involved.

THE CHICKEN STOCK STRATEGY

I will now share with you my favorite investment strategy that will allow you to enjoy the financial benefits stocks can provide, at lower risk. I will show you how to build a Chicken Stock portfolio. These are stocks of companies that have increased their earnings over a long period of time, and have increased their dividends as well. In other words, these companies are increasing profits (thus becoming more valuable) *and* paying you more every year.

Pay attention—this is important!

My exact criteria for Chicken Stocks are very strict within this framework. Companies that meet the Chicken Stock criteria have:

- reported higher profits (earnings) *every quarter* for at least the past 12 years

- passed on their prosperity to their shareholders by issuing higher dividends every year over the same time frame

If you hold stock in companies that meet these Chicken Stock criteria, it puts a safety net under your investments. Even if the market goes down for a while, you'll still receive more dividends every year. Eventually, these payments will force your stock prices higher.

The Chicken strategy is as simple—and as hard—as that. It's *simple* because if you follow the simple rules for selection, you end up with super-strong companies that have performed superbly for investors over long periods of time. It's *hard* because very few people have the discipline to stick with a simple, winning, long-term strategy for many years amidst the distractions of hundreds of other approaches being touted by the expert du jour (of the day).

Warning: Stock market experts can be harmful to your financial health.

ECONOMIC CYCLES

The reason I use 12 years for Chicken Stocks is because, traditionally, we go through three complete economic cycles about every 12 years. In the 12 years immediately preceding the writing of this book, however, we've been in an unusual expansion period. But, this 12-year period has also included recessions, so companies that increased earnings every quarter obviously offered needed goods or services and have good management. In fact, my criteria for Chicken Stocks are so strict that only a handful

STAGES OF ECONOMIC CYCLES

An economic cycle includes four important stages that repeat over time. Chicken Stock prices don't follow these cycles.
1. Expansion
2 Plateau
3. Contraction
4. Trough (recession)

(cycle repeats)

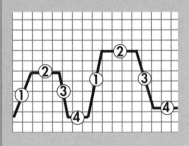

ABBOTT LABORATORIES (ABT)

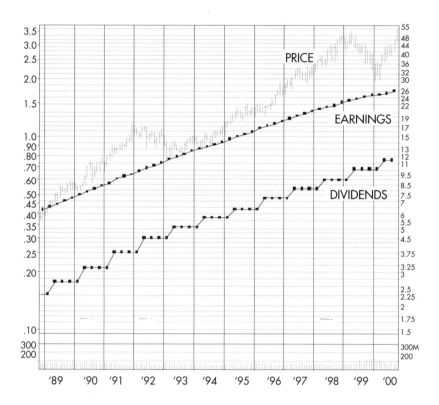

of American stocks qualify out of the thousands available. Some foreign stocks also qualify, but because of currency fluctuations, investing in them involves extra complications.

Because these Chicken Stocks have performed so well and so consistently, they are generally valued more highly than other similar stocks that don't have their consistency. They are never the cheapest stocks in their categories.

One example is Abbott Laboratories. Someone who bought $10,000 worth of Abbot stock in 1990, when the shares sold for $10.50 and the dividend was 22 cents, would have collected a mere $210 in income that year—a 2% yield. But the company has boosted its dividend each year since then. In 2000, that investor would have pocketed 76 cents a share or $700+ for a tidy 7+% yield on the original investment.

At the year 2000 share price of about $45, the original $10,000 of stock is now worth $43,000 (more than four times the initial investment). That's the way to handle the risk of inflation! Of course, Abbott hasn't always gone straight up. As I said, the short-term price is random and unpredictable, but it ultimately follows its earnings and dividends (as shown on the chart on the previous page).

By the way, Abbott is one of the *poorest* of the Chicken Stock performers. If you had invested $10,000 in the Dollar General Corp in 1990, the dividend yield would have been 17+% in December 2000, and your $10,000 initial investment would have grown to $325,500 over that 10-year period.

TECHNOLOGY STOCKS

Technology has been a very popular and volatile sector over the last ten years. Most technology company earnings are too erratic to be Chicken Stocks. And many do not pay dividends, or do not increase dividends regularly. There is, however, one "tech" Chicken Stock—Automatic Data Processing (see chart on the next page).

SHORT-TERM FLUCTUATIONS

As mentioned earlier, the price of a stock at any one point in time is a balance between the supply and demand for that stock. Stock prices can be wildly out of line with any normal way of valuing a company. For instance, if there is a takeover battle underway, the price can go up fast, or, if a company's earnings are expected to go up soon because of a new drug or invention, the stock price may be much higher than justified by the current facts. Over a longer term, though, a stock price is forced upward as dividends and earnings increase. Even if a company was unpopular, if the dividend was higher than other companies, people

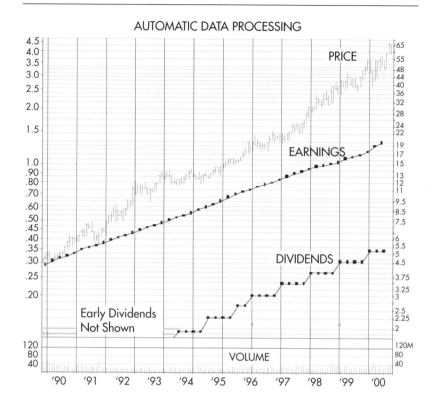

AUTOMATIC DATA PROCESSING

would buy it for the income alone. That's why we say that, over the long term, stock prices reflect the value of the income produced for shareholders.

DIVERSIFICATION

Of course, when employing the Chicken Stock strategy, it's important to diversify your holdings over several stocks, in case one of them falls off the wagon. In other words, any one stock or industry can be hit by some specific problem that may hurt earnings. But when you have different stocks in different industries, you are safer than having all your eggs in one basket. It's also important to monitor the portfolio for any changes that could affect earnings and dividends.

THE CHICKEN STOCK INDEX

To help you follow the performance of Chicken Stocks, I am, for the first time, publicly presenting the Chicken Stock Index. The Chicken Stock Index includes 10 stocks from nine different industries (see the chart below).

The graph on the next page shows the performance of the Chicken Stock index over the 10-year period from May 31, 1991 through May 31, 2001 compared with some of the most popular indexes. An equal investment in all the stocks of the Chicken Index did better than any other index over that period. The NASDAQ index came the closest, but it contained higher-risk stocks.

For a stock to be classified as a Chicken Stock, it must meet several criteria. As mentioned earlier, qualification as a Chicken Stock requires a company to report higher

CHICKEN STOCK PORTFOLIO

Stock	Symbol	Industry
AFLAC Inc.	AFL	Food-Wholesale
Abbott Labs	ABT	Medical supplies
Amer. Int'l Group	AIG	Insurance (life)
Automatic Data Proc.	ADP	Software & svc
General Electric	GE	Electrical equipment
Johnson & Johnson	JNJ	Medical supplies
Sysco Corp.	SYY	Financial services
Wal-Mart Stores	WMT	Retail store
Walgreen Co.	WAG	Drug Store
Wells Fargo	WFC	Bank

GROWTH OF A $10,000 INVESTMENT
FROM MAY 31, 1991 TO MAY 31, 2001

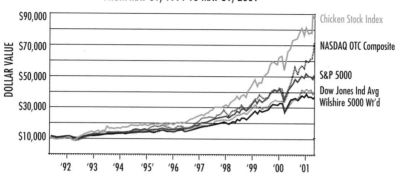

Index	Value	Annualized Return
Chicken Stock Index	$88,166	24.31%
NASDAQ OTC Composite Index	$73,141	22.01%
Standard & Poor's 500 Index	$51,477	17.80%
Dow Jones Industrial Average Index	$40,254	14.94%
Wilshire 5000 Val. Weighted Index	$38,124	14.32%

earnings each quarter and higher dividends each year. However, judgment comes into play when applying this criteria. I do allow occasional situations of lower earnings if they are due to a special unusual circumstance

The higher earnings/higher dividends criteria eliminates many stocks that have seasonal ups and downs in their businesses. For instance, many retailers make the bulk of the year's sales during the Christmas season. A retailer like this may have relatively flat earnings for three quarters of the year (thus disqualifying it as a Chicken Stock). Yet this same retailer may have shown exceptionally strong profits for the fourth quarter over a number of years. Interestingly, Wal-Mart and Dollar General qualify as "Chicken Stocks" with Wal-Mart in the Index.

LOVE THAT CHICKEN:
FINDING CHICKEN STOCKS

For those of you who want to manage your investments on your own, I'll offer suggested resources in many chapters. The easiest places to start are your local library and the Internet.

Many libraries subscribe to expensive services like *Value Line* and the Securities Research Company's *Blue Book of 12-Year Charts.* While these are often available both for the computer and in printed form, most libraries have only the printed versions. These can be slow to use if you want to do a complicated search.

Online resources have a different problem. Many free resources don't provide enough information to conduct complex searches. Also, the trend is for many online resources to charge for use.

How do you find Chicken Stocks? Because of their nature, Chicken Stocks are "blue chip" stocks. But not all blue chips are good enough to be Chicken Stocks.

For example, take one of the "generals" in the Dow Jones Industrial Average, General Motors. Look at the chart on the next page. Does that look like a Chicken Stock to you? Quarterly earnings are all over the place, as are dividends.

BLUE CHIPS?

The dictionary definition of blue chip is a stock issue of high investment quality that usually pertains to a substantial, well-established company and enjoys public confidence in its worth and stability.

According to the folks at word-detective.com, the phrase dates back to 1904, and comes from the blue chips used as the most valuable chips in poker games.

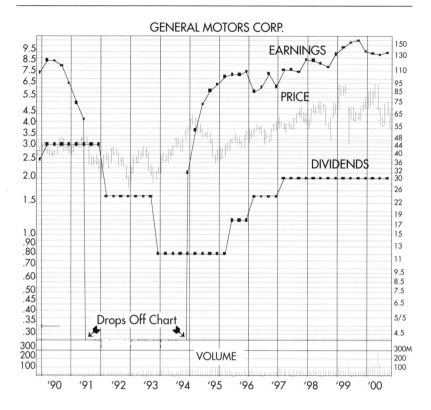

GENERAL MOTORS CORP.

General Motors is considered to be a *cyclical* stock. Compare its performance to Abbott Labs. It's obvious which you should have invested in 12 years ago. As long as the Chicken Stock characteristics continue—higher profits each quarter and higher dividends yearly—it will tend to outperform other blue chips over time.

Take, for example, another "general" of the Dow Jones Industrial Average, General Electric (GE). As you can see from the higher quarterly profits and yearly dividends, it's another Chicken Stock (see chart on the following page). A $10,000 investment 10 years before grew to $109,080 by the end of 2000. The patterns on the stock charts are generally the same for all Chicken Stocks. Once you know what to look for, they are easy to spot.

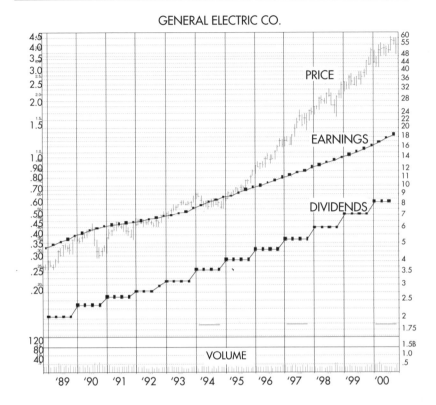

GENERAL ELECTRIC CO.

I like to use the *SRC Blue Book of 12-Year Charts*, published by the Securities Research Company. These are the charts you've seen in this chapter. I like them because they clearly show earnings per share and dividends for each stock over the past 12 years. You can flip through the pages of the chart book while you are relaxing. Stocks with *Chicken* characteristics tend to jump out at you.

Once identified, it's a good idea to research the company further in the *Value Line Survey*. That will cover both earnings and dividends and will tell you more about the company's present financial condition and its future expectations.

Searching for Chicken Stocks online depends on what resources you have available. Value Line will let you search for increased earnings or dividends, or both (www.valueline.com).

SUMMARY

The times truly are "a'changin'," providing you with a longer life expectancy and the financial challenges that go with it. A Chicken Stock portfolio can help you meet those challenges successfully by providing growing income and underlying value. In other words, with this investment strategy, historically, your income has risen along with your principal over time.

4

MUTUAL FUNDS
Mutually Unsatisfying

---

*The average actively managed
stock mutual fund returns approximately
2% less per year to its shareholders
than the stock market returns in general.*
—BILL BARKER, THE MOTLEY FOOL

THE MAJORITY OF MY NEW clients come to me with about 65% of their money in mutual funds. In fact, most individual investors rely heavily on mutual funds, yet the funds aren't doing what people want them to do. For instance, my new clients, the "Chans," were very nervous about the stock market. They held a group of funds whose value had been up and down over the short term. When I looked at their situation, I found two problems:

1 I analyzed the Chan's major holdings with software.

They held 10 different funds with different strategies. This should have given them diversification of their portfolio. But every fund owned many of the same stocks—IBM, Microsoft, and so forth. There had also been "style shifts" in the funds they owned. A style shift means that fund managers advertise a particular style or strategy of management. Then, in response to the market, they change their management style in hopes of getting better short-term performance.

The Chan's financial planner thought their investments were diversified, but they were not. You need to look at the specific stocks held by the fund. Unfortunately, mutual funds only report their holdings quarterly and, by the time they report, they may have made further changes. For instance, all ten of this couple's funds had about 2% in IBM. They were holding more stock in IBM than they had realized.

2 When you buy a mutual fund, you own it with thousands of other people. When more people buy into the fund, you

---

OWNING MULTIPLE MUTUAL FUNDS DOES NOT NECESSARILY PROVIDE DIVERSIFICATION

Let's say you own shares of three different mutual funds. Are your holdings diversified? Probably not. Most funds hold many of the same stocks:

FUND 1	FUND 2	FUND 3
STOCK A	STOCK B	STOCK A
STOCK B	STOCK C	STOCK C
STOCK C	STOCK D	STOCK D

If you held shares of the three funds above, you wouldn't be any more diversified than if you directly held shares of Stocks A, B, C, and D.

are affected whether you like it or not. The new money may force the fund to buy stocks at inappropriately higher prices to keep a predetermined percentage of the overall portfolio (say 2%) in selected stocks. Similarly, when prices go down and other owners redeem their shares, the fund has to sell stocks they may prefer to hold, in order to maintain that 2% level.

In the worst-case scenario, your mutual fund sells their winners and either holds onto their losers or sells them at the wrong time. Like my new clients, the Chans, you can end up with capital gains on which you have to pay taxes, *plus* a loss of share value in your mutual funds.

DIRECT STOCK OWNERSHIP VERSUS MUTUAL FUNDS

I shifted the Chan's portfolio entirely to Chicken Stocks. They can let profits accumulate *untaxed* until they want to sell. They have control over their assets. Their portfolio's performance is up and their average dividened yield is now 8% on their stocks, after five years. Plus, the value of their portfolio has more than doubled.

Invest in Chicken Stocks and you'll receive 100% of your profits and dividends.

At one time, mutual funds were beneficial for the small investor. However, mutual funds create a number of problems. If you can afford to, you are better off owning the stocks directly—that way you'll avoid the problems the Chans encountered.

If you don't have enough money to own the stocks directly, there are specific cases when mutual funds are good, such as for investing in international companies. The next chapter on *unit trusts* also shows you how to get the advantages of mutual funds without most of the drawbacks.

WHAT <u>ARE</u> MUTUAL FUNDS?

Most people have heard of mutual funds. The idea of mutual funds is simple: A mutual fund is a company that invests many people's money in the same investments. Everyone owns the underlying assets together (mutually). Most mutual funds invest in stocks, but there are also mutual funds that invest in bonds, gold, mortgages, and other assets.

> **MUTUAL FUNDS HAVE MULTIPLIED LIKE CRAZY**
>
> Mutual funds were invented in England around 1850. It took them many years to arrive in the United States. They are now so widespread that there are more mutual funds investing in stocks than there are stocks on the New York Stock Exchange.

When a *new* fund is started, the investment company sells shares in the fund to investors. The fund then buys stocks and the investor becomes a part-owner of a large investment portfolio, along with all of the other shareholders of the fund. When you purchase shares of an *existing* fund, the fund manager invests your funds, along with the money contributed by other shareholders, old and new.

To illustrate, let's say I'm going to start a mutual fund. Since it's mine, I'll call it Fred's Mutual Fund. I start with $100,000 and buy the following stocks:

FRED'S MUTUAL FUND
INITIAL PURCHASES

Coca Cola	$20,000
McDonald's	$20,000
Disney	$20,000
IBM	$20,000
Cash (on hand to buy a hot stock—in money market)	$20,000
TOTAL VALUE	**$100,000**

Now my fund is worth $100,000 and I issue 100,000 shares, so each share is worth $1. You buy 100 shares for $100 (plus a tidy commission to me, of course!).

Six months later, the value of the portfolio looks like this:

FRED'S MUTUAL FUND
SIX MONTHS LATER

Coca Cola	$22,000
McDonalds	$20,000
Disney	$23,000
IBM	$24,850
Cash (on hand to buy a hot stock—in money market)	$20,000
Value of Stocks and Cash	**$109,850**
Interest earned	$900
Dividends earned	$2,100
TOTAL VALUE	**$112,850**

Because the value of the stocks has gone up, each share is now worth almost $1.13, until any dividends are paid out. New investors will now have to pay $1.13 for a share of Fred's Mutual Fund. Conversely, if the value of the investments had gone down, each share would be worth less than what you originally paid for it.

You can look in the newspaper to track the values of mutual funds. Most newspapers have a large section devoted to the prices of funds, just as they do to stocks. Here's a sample listing from the paper:

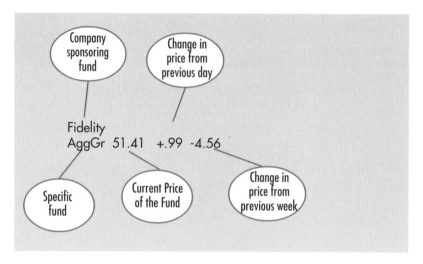

In this case, Fidelity is the main name of the fund. Fidelity has many different funds, however, so there are several listings under the Fidelity heading.

In the example above, the full name of the fund is Aggressive Growth. Its assets were at $51.41 which was up 99¢ for the day and down $4.56 for the past week. Other notations might indicate if there has been a recent dividend, if the fund is new, and if there is a sales load (a sales commission—an extra charge loaded on the buying price!).

WHY MUTUAL FUND COMPANIES HAVE SO MANY DIFFERENT FUNDS —OR— HOW MUTUAL FUNDS ARE LIKE DETERGENTS

Mutual fund companies often have different funds that are invested in particular stock types (such as aggressive growth stocks or utilities). This creates more options for customers—and more management income for the funds!

It's the same principle as Procter & Gamble having many different laundry detergents. If P&G has three of the ten detergents on the grocery store shelf, each of the three brands can appeal to a different type of customer. Additionally, with three of 10 brands owned by P&G, the odds are simply greater that a customer will choose a P&G brand than if only one were on the shelf.

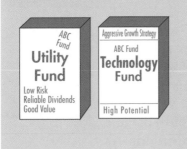

HOW MUTUAL FUND SHARES ARE VALUED

Because shares of most mutual funds are bought and sold every day, prices are tracked in detail, based on the value of the stocks and cash held that day. At the end of each day, the fund calculates the value of all the fund's holdings and then calculates the price of a single share of the fund on that day. You buy new shares at the most recent value (net asset value—NAV).

FUND DISTRIBUTIONS

Mutual funds are required to distribute interest and dividend income to shareholders. Usually, they do this twice a year. You can see this with Fred's Mutual Fund. In the first six months, it earned $3000 in interest and dividends, so each of the 100,000 shares earned 3¢ in addition to the value of a share increasing by almost 10¢.

Toward the end of the year, often in October, a fund pays out the profits they made if they sold any of their stocks or bonds that had gone up in price during that tax year. These profits are *capital gains.*

If it has been a good year with lots of capital gains in a mutual fund, it's often better to buy AFTER the capital gains distribution to avoid taxes. Otherwise, you may pay taxes on gains you didn't receive.

If, during the year, Fred's Mutual Fund sells IBM for a $5000 profit, each of the 100,000 shares would receive 5¢. So, for your hundred shares, you'd receive $5.00. You would report this profit as a capital gain when you file your income tax. Unfortunately, if McDonald's was sold for a $5000 loss, you can't write the loss off on your taxes. All the fund's gains and losses are accumulated over the year—however, sometimes canceling each other out, just as if you held the stocks yourself.

Lack of Tax Planning

Investors can be hit with high taxes when they own mutual funds because they have no control over when stocks get sold. However, relief might lie ahead. There is a bill before Congress that will allow you to defer $3000 a year ($6000 for couples) of your mutual-fund capital-gain distributions, as long as you purchase more mutual fund shares with the money (*reinvest*). While this move reduces the tax bite, it also makes accounting more difficult—you'll have to keep track of which distributions

I have clients with $6,000 in taxable income on a fund that declined 38% in value. "Thrilled" was not one of the words I would use to describe them.
—Terry Seiberlich, a CPA in Walnut Creek, Calif.

you've paid taxes on and which ones you haven't.

The SEC estimates that taxes cost the average mutual fund investor 2.5% a year. Because taxes can significantly reduce your return, the SEC now requires funds to disclose their *after-tax* performance.

OPEN-END FUNDS

The mutual funds I've been describing are *open-ended* funds. Open-ended means that every day the mutual fund management company buys and sells shares with the share price set according to the value of the fund's underlying assets for that day.

If a lot of money comes into the fund in a day, the fund has to decide what to do with the cash. Funds can keep cash on hand, but their policy is to invest it, because the potential earnings on stock investments are much higher than interest on cash holdings. After all, that's why the investor bought the fund—to hold stocks.

If a lot of people sell their shares, the fund has to sell (*liquidate*) some stocks in order to redeem the shares. To illustrate, let's go back to Fred's Mutual Fund again. I did find some hot stocks to invest the cash in, so now Fred's Mutual Fund only has $5000 cash available. Today, several people want to sell their

---

IT'S CORNY YOLK TIME!

Cluck, cluck!

While the US stock market was at an all-time high, the ups and downs frightened a lot of small investors. A guy went to his financial advisor at the bank, who asked if he was worried.

The investor replied that he slept like a baby.

Amazed, the financial advisor asked, "Really? Even with all the fluctuations?"

He said, "Yes. I sleep for a couple of hours, then wake up and cry for a couple of hours."

shares—the combined value of these shares is $10,000. Yikes! I can't pay them—I only have $5000 in cash. The fund's stocks are doing great—I don't want to sell any. But, to pay off the sellers, I am forced to sell $5000 worth of good-performing stocks.

CLOSED-END FUNDS

Closed-end funds do things differently. They raise money for the fund once, and then don't buy or sell any shares. Closed-end funds continue to manage their portfolios of stocks and pay out dividends and capital gains, just as open-end funds do. The shares trade on the market but, in this case, they trade like stocks, with the price depending on supply and demand, *not* the net asset value. So, a share of a closed-end fund might be worth $10 based on the net asset value. But, if the fund's performance has been particularly good, a lot of people are going to be interested in buying shares. With many people seeking to buy a fixed number of shares, the price per share will be bid up. Even though the net asset value is $10, people might be willing to pay $12 for it.

Fund Discounts

In practice, closed-end funds often sell *below* net asset value. The value could be $10, but nobody wants to buy shares right now be-

RECYCLED SALES: AN INCESTUOUS MARKET

There are almost more funds buying stocks than there are stocks to buy. And most funds restrict their purchases to larger capitalization stocks. Thus, most of the big stocks are owned by dozens of mutual funds. This means that part of the daily stock "market" activity is made up of funds selling the same stocks back and forth to each other!

WHY ARE MUTUAL FUNDS SOLD SO FREQUENTLY?

Performance of stocks was great in the 1990s, so mutual funds went up, and many more people became financial planners.

In a bull market, planners boom and mutual funds are "sold" as much as bought. They get lots of publicity. They are easy for brokers and financial planners to sell. In fact, most financial planners are licensed to sell only mutual funds, not stocks. Similarly, 95% of insurance agents can only sell mutual funds. They only need a Series 6 license which is much easier to get. Banks sell mutual funds, too.

cause this is a mutual fund of conservative stocks and everybody wants to buy aggressive stocks. Or, maybe the dividends for this group of stocks have been low. So, if you want to sell your share worth $10, and nobody is willing to pay you $10 for it, you'll have to take whatever someone is willing to pay.

A drawback of closed-end funds is that you can't necessarily cash in your shares and realize their actual net asset value. On the plus side, if you like the portfolio of stocks a closed-end fund holds, you can sometimes purchase these stocks at a discount by buying the fund.

SECTOR FUNDS

Mutual funds that hold stocks in a variety of industries will tend to perform like the general market *minus* fees and expenses. Other mutual funds specialize by investing in a single area or sector such as biotechnology, Internet stocks, or international stocks. These specialized funds lose much of the diversification benefit of mutual funds. They have a high risk. Their sector can do well, as computer stocks did in 1999. They can also do poorly, as biotech stocks did during much of the 1990s, and as Internet stocks did in much of 2000.

Without diversification, your risk can be almost as high in these funds as investing in a single stock.

The advantage is that if you really like a sector such as telecommunications, but you aren't sure which stock to buy, a *sector fund* is a safer way to go.

ADVANTAGES OF MUTUAL FUNDS

There are a number of advantages to owning mutual funds:
- diversification
- professional management and expertise
- access to investments you couldn't otherwise afford as an individual
- bookkeeping, IRA forms
- families of funds

Diversification

The most important way to reduce your risk in the stock market is *diversification*. By owning multiple stocks in multiple industries, you avoid problems that may affect one company or one industry. Much of the up and down variation that most people define as risk is smoothed out by diversification. Mutual funds do a better job of diversification than almost any individual investor because they can own hundreds of different stocks. This is less true of mutual funds that specialize in an industry (sector funds). In that case, you have diversi-

A SAMPLING OF A FEW OF THE MANY DIFFERENT MUTUAL FUNDS OFFERED BY ONE FIRM (AIM)

- Aggressive Growth
- Basic Value
- Blue Chip
- Capital Development
- Developing Markets
- Emerging Growth
- European Small Company
- Global Aggressive Growth
- Global Utilities
- High Yield
- Income Fund
- International Equity
- Japan Growth
- Money Market
- Municipal Bond
- New Technology

For details: www.aimfunds.com.

fication from the risk of a single company, but not an industry.

If you have $1000 to invest and you invest it all in Coca Cola, your money rises or falls depending on that one stock. If Coca Cola has a good year, great, you've made a profit. But, if there happens to be a case of product tampering that causes a national scare, or the price of sugar goes up, investors are scared off and the stock price can plummet. Your $1000 might now be worth $500. If, instead, you had invested in a mutual fund that owned Coca Cola as well as a number of other stocks, the impact of Coca Cola's drop in price would be offset (hopefully) by gains in the other stocks held. In the example below, you can see that, when Coca Cola was only 20% of your portfolio and the price dropped by half, you ended up losing only $100 instead of $500.

On the down side, mutual funds also tend to average out big gains. If your $1000 of Coca Cola rose to $1500, you'd be very happy. You'd be $500 ahead. But, if you had invested in a mutual fund that included Coca Cola, that big gain would be brought down by any losses in other stocks. Portfolios of stocks tend to perform like the market. As you see in the chart on the next page, Coca Cola's 50% rise in price that gave you a $500 profit is brought down to a $100 profit when mixed in with other stocks with losses and moderate gains.

SHOULD YOU BUY MUTUAL FUNDS SHARES OR BUY STOCK IN THE COMPANY THAT SELLS YOU THE FUNDS?

If a company offers mutual funds, would you be better off buying shares of the mutual fund or would you be better off buying shares of the company itself? Research shows that mutual fund companies typically make more money managing your money than their funds make for you!

HOLDING COCA COLA AS AN INDIVIDUAL...

	INITIAL PRICE	COKE PRICE FALLS	COKE PRICE RISES
Coca Cola (5 shares)	$200	$100	$300
TOTAL	$1000	$500	$1500

HOLDING COCA COLA IN A MUTUAL FUND...

MUTUAL FUND PURCHASES	INITIAL PRICE	COKE PRICE FALLS	COKE PRICE RISES
Coca Cola	$200	$100	$300
Stock 2	200	150	150
Stock 3	200	220	220
Stock 4	200	220	220
Stock 5	200	210	210
TOTAL	$1000	$900	$1100

Professional Management

Professional managers make up for two weaknesses of individual investors. They provide expertise and time. By managing millions of dollars, mutual funds can afford to hire people with training and experience in the stock market. You receive the benefit of their stock selections. They can spend full time watching the market and researching individual companies. So professional managers *should* get even smarter over time. While "professional" fund

Mr. Fund Manager, this stock shows just the fundamentals you wanted!

managers do have expertise, often the people actually doing the research are youngsters only a few years out of school.

While you might expect that professional managers would do better than the overall market, on average, they do worse. Since professional managers account for the bulk of stock market trading, their overall performance is generally going to be close to the market average; most do worse than average when their fees are taken into account.

Access to Investments

Because they control millions, or even billions of dollars, mutual funds can buy many investments that you cannot. For instance, the shares of Berkshire Hathaway, run for many years by the famous investor Warren Buffet, cost about $10,000 each at one point. Most individual investors cannot afford to buy many shares at this price. There are also investments like *corporate paper* issued $100,000 at a time. And you've probably heard about how hard it is to buy initial public offerings (IPOs) of new stocks when stocks are hot. Most of those shares are reserved for investors with "connections," and many of those shares doubled the first day. That means that, if you got the stock at the original IPO price, you could make lots of money reselling them later. In

---

DON'T BUY LAST YEAR'S "HOT" FUND

By chance, a small percentage of funds will beat the market each year. But with mutual funds, past performance does not predict future performance.

Burton G. Malkiel, author of *A Random Walk Down Wall Street*, says, "Most investors would be considerably better off by purchasing a low-expense index fund than by trying to select an active fund manager who appears to possess a 'hot hand.'"

David Dreman, author of *The New Contrarian Investment Strategy*, concurs: "How quickly investors flock to better-performing mutual funds, even though financial researchers have shown that the 'hot' funds in one time period very often turn out to be the poorest performers in another."

general, mutual funds are in a better position to get these in-demand investments than you are as an individual.

Financial Records

If you were to own a lot of stocks on your own, keeping track of all the financial records could become complicated. Mutual funds do all the bookkeeping and send you a simple summary for tax, IRA, and other purposes.

Families of Funds

Because so many companies manage many different mutual funds, you can switch your investment from one to another at no, or minor, cost. For instance, you could switch from a stock to a bond fund, or from a high-tech to a general fund. This allows you to respond to changing market conditions or your personal circumstances.

Other Advantages

A few other advantages of mutual funds are listed from time to time, such as automatic investment programs, emotional detachment from day-to-day decisions, and so forth. These advantages, however, are generally minor—nobody buys a mutual fund because of them.

DRAWBACKS OF MUTUAL FUNDS

Fees

One of the advantages of mutual funds—professional management—also creates some disadvantages. A big disadvantage is professional fees. While great management

> ...the results [of a study on mutual fund performance] do not support the existence of skilled or informed mutual fund portfolio managers.
> —Mark M. Cathcart, USC, in *Journal of Finance*

can be a big advantage, the fact that the majority of mutual funds are estimated to do worse than the market after fees are taken into account makes you wonder what you're getting for your money. If fund management takes only 1% a year, the compounding effect makes it hard to beat the market.

Professional managers running thousands of mutual funds and pension funds create most of the market through their buying and selling, so it's hard for them to beat themselves. From the investor's point of view, why pay for management when you can simply buy a *market index fund* with lower fees that equals the overall market performance (which is better than most mutual funds)? [Index funds are described on the next page.]

TAX IMPLICATIONS

Another problem with mutual funds is that, by law, they must distribute income and capital gains to shareholders every year. This can hurt your tax planning. You may have to report some gains as ordinary income. When you hold stocks yourself, you can defer gains until you want them.

I'm proud to be paying taxes in the United States. The only thing is, I could be just as proud for half the money. —ARTHUR GODFREY

Size Limitations

Because mutual funds handle billions of dollars, they must trade only in the largest stocks. Even if they bought a $15 stock, and the stock doubled, it wouldn't influence the value of a billion-dollar fund. Since many of the big percentage gains among stocks are in smaller companies, mutual funds miss out on these growth investments.

The Rich Get Poorer

As funds do better, they attract more money, further restricting the size of stocks they can buy. This means that any fund that has great performance is going to attract lots of new money. Many times, the types of stocks they bought last year that performed well aren't available any more at the right price, so the new money gets invested in other types of stocks. The larger the fund, the more they are forced to invest like everyone else, because they "become" the general market. Therefore, the funds that do exceptionally well one year tend to do worse the next, especially if they are investing in narrow sectors of the markets, rather than across the board.

INDEX FUNDS/INDEX SHARES

In one year, 85% of all mutual funds failed to do better than the average of the *Standard & Poor's 500 (S&P 500)* stocks.

Since most mutual funds do not do as well as the market, *index funds* were developed to *match* the market. An index fund buys stock in all the companies of a particular index, thereby reproducing the performance of an entire section of the market.

The most popular stock market index is the Standard & Poor's 500, but there are index funds that track about 30 different indexes, and more are added all the time. The main ones are the Dow Jones Industrial Average, and NASDAQ. But there are dozens of others such as Value Line and the *Wilshire 5000.*

In theory, these funds should always match the market exactly. In practice, some funds do not exactly match the markets they are indexing, so you need to check their track record. While investing in a stock index fund means that you'll do about as well as the overall market, it also guarantees that you'll never *outperform* the overall market.

Because there are few management decisions to make in an index fund, management fees are low. A stock index fund has no need for highly-paid stock analysts. The hard parts about running a mutual fund are gone—stock selection and timing of buying and selling. Those savings in lower fees can be passed along to investors in the form of higher total returns.

MUTUAL FUND VERSUS INDEX FUND PERFORMANCE

John C. Bogle, chairman of The Vanguard Group of Investment Companies, sums it up well in his foreword to W. Scott Simon's book, *Index Mutual Funds:* "Over the past 25 years, the average fund had annual returns averaging 11.6% compared to a return of 13.1% for Standard & Poor's 500 Stock Index. This is a shortfall of 1.5% per year...And simple arithmetic makes it clear that this difference is critically important. Over 25 years, a $10 investment in the Index would have risen in value to $217,100, compared to $155,500 in the average mutual fund. The shortfall—$61,000—is clearly enormous.... Costs matter. That sums up the case for index funds."

"INDEX" STOCKS (EXCHANGE-TRADED FUNDS)

In addition to regular, open-ended index mutual funds, there are also closed-end index funds bought and sold like stocks. The first were Standard & Poor's Depository Receipts (SPDRs—pronounced "spiders"). Depository receipts mean that there are actual *shares on deposit.* In the case of Spiders, shares of all 500 stocks in the Standard and Poor's Index are held on deposit. The similar instrument for the Dow Jones is usually referred to as *Diamonds* (DIA) and this type of investment is called an *exchange-traded fund* (ETF) in general.

Advantages of ETFs

Unlike mutual funds, ETFs are shares of stock themselves. You buy and sell them on the stock exchange. These new Index shares mirror exactly the value of the underlying shares making up the index. In other words, the Standard and Poor's Index consists of 500 shares of the 500 companies making up the index. If the average value of these shares were $10, one complete Index would cost $5,000. Since this is a high price for a share of stock to trade at, Spiders are issued to represent one-tenth of the total index. Thus, one S&P Spider share would be priced at $500.

Investors pay an estimated $68 billion a year to have funds pick and hold stocks for them. What do they get for all this money? Not a lot.

— James W. Michaels, *Forbes* magazine

This is an example of the markets creatively making up new products to sell. While index mutual funds and Spiders are similar, if they both reflect the S&P 500, there are some differences. They are:

- purchasing
- market fluctuations
- other vehicles
- variety
- cost

Purchasing

Index mutual funds are bought directly from the fund. Minimum investments are usually $2,000–3,000. ETFs can be bought through any broker. That means you could buy as little as one share for, say, $500. But a "round lot" of 100 shares would cost about $50,000.

Market Fluctuations

Spiders are for sale all day, anytime markets trade. So prices will go up and down during the day, and you can sell anytime during the day at that price. Index funds are priced, and all transactions entered, only *once at the end of each day.* Though you can decide to buy or sell anytime, your transaction will wait to be fulfilled until the end of the day, *and* at the end of the day's price.

Other Vehicles

ETFs can be sold short, have options written against them, or anything else you can do with stock. Mutual funds are not as flexible. If you are buying an index mutual fund, you normally wouldn't want to trade it quickly, and you could not sell short. Your goal in an index fund should be to conservatively match the market.

Variety

There are more exchange-traded funds than index funds. For example, ETFs are available for sections of the S&P index, the Dow, and foreign stocks.

Cost

ETFs tend to cost more in total fees and brokerage commissions than Index funds.

FOR THE DO-IT-YOURSELF INVESTOR

The easiest way to research mutual funds is to use www.Morningstar.com or *Forbes* magazine's annual issue on mutual funds (www.forbes.com). Between these two sources, you can select funds of any kind. *Forbes* rates fund performance in both up and down markets. Thus, a rare AA fund would be a best performer in both markets.

SUMMARY

Mutual funds are very popular and are sold by many people. Unfortunately, many never match the performance of the overall market, although they can provide diversification. If you want to track the major markets, an index mutual fund is probably the most cost-effective way. If you want to do more complex activities like shorting, hedging, or spreading (for definitions, see the glossary), or invest in foreign indexes, ETFs are often best. There is another often-overlooked investment that gives you many of the advantages of mutual funds without many of the drawbacks. The next chapter will cover these "unit trusts," which I generally prefer to mutual funds.

5

TRUST IN
UNIT TRUSTS

---

*Equity unit investment trusts just might turn out to be
the mutual funds of the new millennium. This is
cutting-edge stuff.*
—Doug Fabian, Investment newsletter publisher

MUTUAL FUNDS USE MONEY FROM
many people to obtain better diversification of a stock portfolio, to achieve econo-
mies of scale, and to hire full-time, professional management. These benefits are
what attract the majority of investors. Most
people, however, don't know there's a better way—unit investment trusts (UITs).

Unit investment trusts were invented
in Scotland in the mid-1800s and first in-
troduced in this country by the John
Nuveen Company in 1961. UITs are like a

mutual fund in that they buy a diversified group of stocks or bonds according to a specified strategy. But UITs differ significantly from mutual funds in a number of ways, and these differences make them the better choice for most investors. The basic difference is that unit trusts use a *buy-and-hold strategy*. Unlike mutual funds, you actually own the underlying group of stocks you initially acquire for the life of the trust (usually from one to five years).

> Unit investment trusts are fixed over the life of the trust. There is no trading of the portfolio.

UNIT TRUSTS VERSUS MUTUAL FUNDS

The advantages of unit trusts over open-ended mutual funds are the same as you receive when buying a stock directly. By buying and holding at one price, when the stock goes up, you make all of the profits, instead of sharing them with others.

Unit trusts give you the advantage of owning a large portfolio of stocks directly, without having to spend millions of dollars to buy them. A unit trust is a legal form that segregates your ownership and protects you from the influences of what other buyers and sellers do. When you own a unit trust, you do not own the shares "mutually" with thousands of other investors. In a mutual fund, when other investors panic and sell the fund, your shares are being sold too. And, as discussed in the last chapter, when a mutual fund is popular, the new money coming in raises your average cost of the winning shares.

> Put not your trust in money, but put your money in trust.
> —Oliver Wendell Holmes

WHY WERE UITs DEVELOPED?

UITs were originally developed for bonds. Bond Unit Investment Trusts made perfect sense for a buy-and-hold strategy. If you couldn't afford to buy a number of different bonds to achieve the safety of diversification, you could afford to buy "units" of a trust that did.

Bonds expiring about the same time would be purchased for the portfolio, and the fund would expire when the bonds did. During the life of the fund, regular bond interest rates would be paid out. Then, upon expiration, your capital was returned. At that time, you could put your money into a new trust if you wished to remain invested. Management selects the portfolio, but then does not need to actively manage it during its lifetime. This means relatively low management fees.

Eventually, Unit Investment Trusts were used for stocks, and their growth has been tremendous. In 1990, investors put $7 billion into bond unit trusts and less than $1/2 billion into stock unit trusts. In the year 2000, about $2 billion went into bond unit trusts while about *$100 billion* went into stock unit trusts! In 1998 alone, the number of stock unit trusts doubled.

What really kicked off the use of UITs for stocks was an old strategy called "Dogs of the Dow." Only rich investors could afford to buy a significant number of shares of the top ten dividend-paying stocks in the Dow Jones Industrial Average. This strategy beat the averages for many years. Once a unit trust allowed smaller investors to do the same thing with as little as $1000, the strategy took off and so did stock unit trusts.

DOGS OF THE DOW

This strategy involves putting an equal amount of money into each of the top-10 highest-yielding stocks of the Dow Jones Industrial Average at the beginning of every year. Hold for a year. At the end of one year, reconfigure your portfolio so you have the current top-10 dividend-payers again. I've used this strategy myself in the past. I've stopped using it, however, because it seems to be less effective lately.

ADVANTAGES OF UNIT TRUSTS

Here are the advantages unit trusts offer over mutual funds:
- a more clearly defined focus (for instance, unit trusts cover companies from a specific area of the country, implement specific strategies, or cover narrow sectors or regions where there are not comparable mutual funds)
- lower management costs because the portfolio is fixed, not changing
- your holdings are not affected if others buy or sell their units

- you are not forced to pay capital gains at unexpected times determined by management
- predictable dividend income, because the stocks in the portfolio are fixed
- a planned holding period (this can provide discipline during market ups and downs when emotions can cause buying and selling at the wrong times)
- sales commissions are often spread over time, so more of your money goes to work up front
- in-kind distribution (many UITs will let you trade your units for the shares they hold in the trust— this allows you to extend your holding period for the investment)

DISADVANTAGES OF UNIT TRUSTS

Of course, there are a few disadvantages to unit trusts as well. The main one is that some may be hard to sell before the expiration date if they are issued by a *small* investment firm. Commissions can also be high, depending on the trust. And if market conditions change, your unit trust may be less flexible than a mutual fund that can adjust its portfolio.

HIGH TECH INVESTING FOR COWARDS

One area of the stock market that is attractive but has been very volatile (lots of ups and downs) is the technology sector. There have been opportunities to make a lot of money, but there have been "black holes" along the way. It's hard to pick specific stocks in high technology. Because advances are happening so fast in this industry, a technology company can become a dinosaur in two years. So, a more conservative way for "cowards" is to own the whole group.

Specific Technology Examples

If you're a "coward" but you want to buy volatile high technology stocks, unit trusts are the more conservative way to do it. One of my favorite approaches to the volatile tech sector is to buy a unit trust. My favorite such unit trust is the 35 stocks of the *Morgan Stanley High-Tech 35 Index.* You can buy this from any broker or online. It's composed not only of NASDAQ stocks, but contains stocks from the Dow Jones Industrial Average as well. It even has one Chicken Stock in it (ADP). The advantage of this approach is that you will own stocks that represent almost every aspect of the technology sector. As one example, the box on the opposite page shows a list of the stocks, grouped by sector, in one offering of this unit trust.

Another unit trust for high tech that I like is called the *NASDAQ Strategic 10.* These unit trusts are created by Van Kampen & Co. Their strategy for picking the ten stocks is very disciplined. The Strategic 10 stocks are selected from the twenty biggest nonfinancial companies listed on NASDAQ. They are the ten companies with the highest annual sales in the last year. These ten companies are usually high tech ones. An equal dollar amount is then invested in each company. For example, in one portfolio in 2001, these 10 stocks were:

- MCI Worldcom, Inc.
- Intel
- Dell Computers

MORGAN STANLEY HIGH-TECHNOLOGY 35*

Computer Business & Software
Automatic Data Processing
Electronic Data Systems
First Data Corporation

Enterprise Software/Technical Software
Computer Associates Intl.
Oracle Corp.
Parametric Technology
PeopleSoft, Inc.

Internet & PC Software
Amazon.com, Inc.
America Online, Inc.
Electronic Arts
Intuit, Inc.
Microsoft Corp.
Yahoo! Inc.

Semiconductors
Intel Corp.
Micron Technology, Inc.
STMicroelectronics N.V.
Texas Instruments, Inc.
Xilinx, Inc.

PC Hardware & Data Storage
Compaq Computer
Dell Computer
Palm, Inc.
Seagate Technology, Inc.

Electronics Manufacturing Services
Solectron Corp.

Networking & Telecom Equipment
Broadcom Corp.
Cisco Systems, Inc.
JDS Uniphase
Lucent Technologies, Inc.
Motorola, Inc.
Nortel Networks Corp.
Tellabs

Server & Enterprise Hardware
EMC Corp.
Hewlett-Packard
IBM
Sun Microsystems

Semiconductor Capital Equipment
Applied Materials

* Categories and stocks listed in the November 2000 prospectus.

- LM Ericsson
- Microsoft Corp.
- Cisco Systems, Inc.
- Sun Microsystems
- Oracle Corp.
- Applied Materials, Inc.
- Comcast Corp.

Many other investment companies such as Nike, Nuveen,and Ranson also assemble unit trusts.

FOR THE DO-IT-YOURSELF INVESTOR

The Web sites of the major sellers of unit trusts are the best places to start your research. These include: www.nikesec.com, www.nuveen.com, www.ranson.com, and www.vankampen.com. For general information on unit trusts, try www.uitnet.com.

SUMMARY

I've suggested in this chapter that unit investment trusts are newer and more sophisticated investment vehicles. They can give you better control and results than "your father's mutual funds." If you want to invest by following specific strategies, I prefer unit trusts over mutual funds for implementing them.

As of the writing of this book, unit trusts are relatively unknown compared to mutual funds. I still like mutual funds in some situations. For 401(k)s and foreign stocks, mutual funds are more practical. They fit 401(k) requirements better. And they work better for foreign stocks because you need active management and currency hedging. But, for most other situations, unit investment trusts are clearly the winner.

6

GENTLEMEN
PREFER BONDS

An honest man's word is as good as his bond.
—CERVANTES (*DON QUIXOTE*)

WHEN THE COHENS, A RETIRED couple, came to me, all of their money—a rollover from their pension plan—had been put in a government bond fund. They invested in bonds because they wanted their investment to be super safe. They also wanted to maintain their principal while drawing enough money to live on.

Unfortunately, by the end of a year, not only had their dividends dropped, but their principal went down about 20%. The value of their investment had shrunk from

Note: "Gentlemen prefer bonds" was first said by Andrew Mellon, US Treasury Secretary, during the Crash of 1929.

$400,000 to $320,000. They were scared and didn't know what to do. I recommended that they invest in Chicken Stocks (see page 103 for why bond funds are so dangerous). After one year in Chicken Stocks, both their income and principal rose above where they first started. Now they are receiving even more income, and their net worth is higher than ever.

A chapter on bonds is included in this book, not because I like bonds, but for those people who need more immediate income than stocks can generate.

Bonds are valuable when you need more income *now*. The long-term problem with bonds is that they will not do what properly selected stocks will do. First, most bonds won't keep up with inflation. Second, bonds won't grow your assets over the long term. Many times, you will be better off buying stocks and selling some every year for income than you would be in bonds.

I recommend that you use only as many bonds as necessary for immediate income. Put the rest of your investments in Chicken Stocks, which can keep up with inflation plus grow your assets and income.

WHAT ARE BONDS?

Many people aren't really sure what bonds are. (If you already know the basics of bonds, you may want to skip to page 103.) Bonds are simply IOUs. When you buy a bond, you are making a loan to the *bond issuer.* The bond issuer promises to pay a particular interest rate for a fixed period of time, then your principal is returned.

Let's say the XYZ Widget Company wants to upgrade their production equipment because they then could produce widgets 50% faster. To get the money for this, they issue 100 $1000 bonds. The bonds pay 8% and are due in seven years. If you buy a bond for $1000, XYZ Widget will pay you 8% interest a year, and at the end of the seven years will repay your $1000. Interest is generally paid twice a year until the date the bond principal—the loan—is due.

Bonds are as safe as the borrower issuing them (or their guarantor). So, US government bonds are safer than corporate bonds.

Corporate bonds are issued in units of $1000 face value each. Government bonds can come in other amounts, such as the various types of savings bonds. You've probably voted on various local and state bond issues in your area to raise money for schools, prisons, the environment, or other public projects (municipal bonds). If the bond issue receives a positive vote, the state or municipality is authorized to sell bonds to finance the project. When you purchase a new bond, you are lending money to the issuer, whether it be a company or government agency.

"Hey, how come these US Corporate Bonds I bought are written in Chinese?"

There is also a bond "market" where you can purchase bonds issued previously.

When you purchase a bond through the market, it is generally being resold by someone else—it is not a new issue. Just as with stocks, it is this reselling of bonds that makes up most of the market activity. The fact that you can resell a bond easily makes them a "liquid" investment. In fact, the worldwide market for bonds is generally much larger than the market for stocks.

WHY DO PEOPLE BUY BONDS?

We know that bonds are sold to raise money for projects, but why would people buy them? In World War II, War Bonds (issued to finance the war effort) were often purchased for patriotic reasons.

HOW SAVINGS BONDS WORK

Savings bonds work somewhat differently than regular bonds. Rather than be paid interest at regular intervals, you buy savings bonds at a discounted rate. Then, at the end of the term, you redeem them for their full value. Thus, you might pay about $35 for a $50 savings bond. At the end of eight years, the bond is bought back for $50.

Savings bonds continue to accrue interest after they are due (for up to 40 years depending on the bond and date of issue), so if you redeem your $50 bond ten years after the due date, you might receive $75. (Visit www.publicdebt.treas.gov/sav/savcalc.htm to use a calculator that will determine the current value of your savings bonds.)

Today, most people buy bonds because they want to receive a higher rate of interest than they could get from a bank. Bond interest is higher than bank interest because, when you buy a bond, you are lending money directly to the end user. Banks usually pay less interest because they are "middlemen"—they take their profits from loaning your money to others. In order to attract investors, companies that issue the bonds have to pay high enough interest to be competitive with banks.

Tax-Free Possibilities

You've heard of the *national debt*—that is simply all the money the US government owes because of bonds it has sold to raise money (plus money borrowed from sources like Social Security). This extra money from the sales of bonds lets the government spend more than it collects in taxes. Even when the government balances the budget, it continues to sell some bonds to ensure a flow of new money to pay off some of the older bonds.

> ### CLIPPING COUPONS
>
> You may have heard the old expression "clipping coupons." That expression comes from bonds issued in days of yore. If you had bought a bond from XYZ Widgets in 1900, the bond would come with interest coupons attached. When an interest payment was due, you had to cut off a coupon and send it in to receive your interest. So if you're reading a book that says the gentleman didn't work but clipped coupons, now you'll know that the gentleman wasn't clipping "10¢ off" coupons for toilet paper, but rather was wealthy enough to live off the interest payments on his bonds.

Interest paid on US government bonds is generally free of state and local taxes. Many state and local bonds (municipals) are free of federal taxes, as well as state, and local taxes. Since what you take home *after taxes* is your actual profit, this means that tax-free government bonds can pay a lower rate of interest and still be competitive with corporate bonds. It is a tax shelter designed to help governments raise money at a lower cost.

The example here shows how tax-free bonds can pay you less interest, but still put more money in your pocket after taxes:

	XYZ Widget Corporate Bond	Local Municipal Tax-Free Bond
Bond cost	$1000	$1000
Interest rate	8%	7%
Interest paid	$80	$70
Tax rate	25%	0
After-tax profit	$60	$70

TYPES OF BONDS

Zero-Coupon Bonds

Zero-coupon bonds are bonds that pay no interest until the final redemption date. Like government savings bonds, they are sold for less than face value, to include their interest if you hold them until maturity. For example, for $500 you may buy a bond with a face value of $1000. You might buy this kind of bond if you didn't need current income and didn't want the small interest payments along the way. Because money is worth more now than later, zero-coupon bonds may also pay a slightly higher rate than bonds that pay interest along the way.

A subtle advantage of zero-coupon bonds is that they pay interest on their interest during the entire life of the bond. This means that you receive the same rate of interest on all your money. With regular bonds, you may not be able to reinvest the interest they pay at the same rate, if interest rates have gone down by the time you receive your payment. (This is called reinvestment risk.) A disadvantage is that you have to pay taxes on interest as it accumulates all during the life of the bond, even though you don't actually get the money until the bond comes due.

Treasuries

US government bonds are often called Treasuries, since they are issued by the Treasury Department to raise money for the government. They are considered the safest bonds available and are exempt from state and local taxes. They are the safest because it is extremely unlikely that our government would fail (and if it did, a few defaulted bonds would probably be the least of our worries!).

Treasury bills have short-term maturities, from four weeks to a year. The terms for *Treasury notes* range from one to five years (although one-year notes are now seldom issued). As mentioned earlier, they are sold at a discount from face value and are paid off in full at maturity. *Treasury bonds* are for terms from five to about 20 years (30-year bonds are occasionally available).

I-Bonds

The *I-bond* is a Treasury bond that was first issued in the last part of the 1990s. This bond was created to address the problem of inflation. Bonds are riskier than they look because they don't protect you against inflation (I'll talk about this in more detail later in this chapter). The "I" in I-bond stands for "inflation-indexed" because the interest paid by the bond is adjusted for inflation. When I-bonds were first issued, they weren't particularly popular, but they have gained in popularity, depending on current inflation rates.

The rate I-bonds pay has two parts. The "core" rate is expected to be the after-inflation return on the loan to the government. The "floating" rate varies to equal inflation. For instance at one point in 2000, the core rate of interest was 3.4% and the "floating rate"—that part adjusted for inflation—was 3.82%. That would mean that if inflation was 3.82%, you'd still end up with 3.4% after-inflation interest on your bond. In other words, you are guaranteed to receive the core interest rate, no matter what the inflation rate is.

BONUS INTEREST FOR I-BOND HOLDERS

The government surprised people in Spring 2000 by raising the core rate on I-bonds from 3.4% to 3.6%. The government doesn't have to do this—the original rate is guaranteed not to go down; there are no promises to raise the rate if interest rates go up. However, the government raised the rate to a combined rate of 7.42 to be more competitive with other bonds offered, in order to sell more bonds.

Government Agency Bonds

A number of federal agencies (or quasi-agencies) also issue bonds separately, especially for housing loans. These include the Government National Mortgage Association (Ginnie Mae), and others nicknamed Fannie Mae and Freddie Mac. These agencies pay slightly higher interest rates than Treasuries, even though they are backed by the government.

Municipal Bonds

Municipal bonds are issued by cities, states, and their agencies. They are usually free from federal, state, and local taxes. These bonds vary in risk.

"General obligation" municipal bonds are the lowest risk because the city, for instance, can collect taxes to pay them, if needed. Only a very few cities have ever gone bankrupt and not paid their bonds.

"Revenue bonds" are supported by the income

> ### WHEN MUNICIPAL BONDS AREN'T TAX FREE
>
> Municipal bonds aren't always tax free. Federal laws prohibit municipalities from issuing tax-free bonds for projects such as sports stadiums that don't benefit the general public.
>
> To compensate for the loss of tax-free status, interest rates are generally higher on these taxable municipal bonds. These bonds, however, are often exempt from state and local taxes. This makes them a better deal than similarly rated corporate bonds (and, municipalities are safer).

from the project for which they are used. For instance, if a city's stadium is financed by revenue bonds, a portion of the stadium rent and other revenue will be used to pay off the bonds. If the project doesn't generate enough income, the bonds may not be paid off. For extra safety, many municipal bonds are insured. However, in keeping with the principle that safer bonds pay less interest, insured bonds pay a little less interest.

Corporate Bonds

Corporate bonds make up the majority of bonds. They are issued by thousands of different companies and vary in risk. They pay higher interest than the various government bonds that are considered safer. How high a rate depends on how stable the corporate finances are and the general level of interest rates at the time.

Bearer Bonds

Bearer bonds are a type of bond that is not registered to a particular person. Whoever holds them, owns them. Because there's not much of a paper trail with bearer bonds, the Tax Reform Act of 1982 outlawed their use. Even so, there are bearer bonds that remain in circulation. Also, some foreign countries still issue bearer bonds. Bearer bonds have coupons. Since bearer bonds aren't registered in your name, the company doesn't know to whom the interest is due, so twice a year you have to "clip a coupon" and send it in to collect your interest.

BEARER BONDS GO HOLLYWOOD

Because bearer bonds can be cashed in by whomever is in possession of them, they often crop up in movies. For instance, in *Die Hard* (starring Bruce Willis), the criminals pretended to be terrorists taking hostages, in order to steal $640 million in bearer bonds. Here are a few other movies in which bearer bonds play a role:

- *Beverly Hills Cop* (1979)
- *Cliffhanger* (1993)
- *Heartwood* (1998)
- *Heat* (1995)
- *Shaft* (2000)

BEARER BOND HEIST

READING BOND PRICE TABLES

While I do NOT encourage you to worry about daily, or even monthly, changes in bond prices, reading the price tables in your local paper is much like reading the stock tables. Many newspapers do not list bonds daily, or only list samples, so you may have to go to the library or subscribe to an investment newspaper to find them.

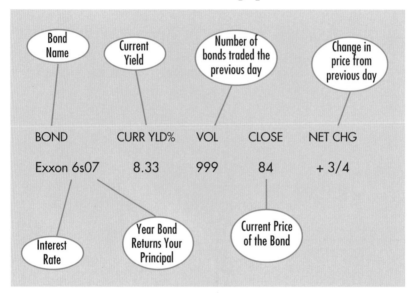

BOND	CURR YLD%	VOL	CLOSE	NET CHG
Exxon 6s07	8.33	999	84	+ 3/4

In the sample above, the bond name comes first. Names are usually abbreviations. Because they are in alphabetical order (sometimes by the exchange they sell on), you should be able to find your company. In this case, Exxon is the full name of the oil company.

Immediately after the name of the bond is the interest rate and the year it pays back the principal (when it expires or matures). In this case, it pays 6% a year and matures in 2007.

The next two columns are the current yield based on the traded price of the bond (8.33%), and the volume of bonds traded (999).

The next column is the current price of the bond (with one zero taken off: 84 = $840). While it is worth $1000 when it matures, current prices will go up or down depending on interest rates. If the prices on old bonds didn't adjust to produce the current yield, nobody would buy them compared to newer bonds. In this case, the 8.33%

yield is produced by lowering the price of the bond to $840. Your bond can also adjust up in price if it pays more than the current interest rate.

The last column is the change in the bond's price from the previous day, up or down. In this case, it is 3/4, so the previous day's price must have been 83¼. The price usually changes a smaller amount each day than the price of a stock of comparable value would. Because of this smaller range of variation, bonds are considered less risky than stocks.

BASIC BOND SAFETY

Most bonds are sold by companies to raise money without giving up *equity* (stock). If the company whose bond you buy is strong, its bonds are very safe. They pay interest when it is due and, when the bond matures, they pay back the face value ($1000).

Even if the company has problems and goes out of business, the bond holders have first claim against the assets of the company. Sometimes, however, your full $1000 loan is not repaid if the value of the assets is not enough to cover the costs of redeeming all of the outstanding bonds.

As we discussed in Chapter 1, and will discuss further in the next section of this chapter, bonds are not really less risky in the long term when you consider inflation and the purchasing value of your dollars.

Junk bonds, which received so much attention in the 1980s, are bonds of companies that are considered financially weak or are unrated. Even in those cases, about 95% of bonds were repaid, so there has not been much risk of loss. Even so, there are other risks in bonds.

PRICE FLUCTUATION RISK

If you sell a bond early—before it expires and pays off the $1000 loan—you may not get all of your money back. Since bonds are purchased for the interest payments, their price goes up and down every day with interest rates. If you bought a bond that pays 5% and then interest rates go up to 10% on new bonds, you would lose about half your money if you sold early because all new buyers would expect 10% on the money they invest. The table shows how this works.

YEAR BOUGHT	NAME	PRICE OF BOND	INTEREST RATE (Original Rate)	YEARLY INTEREST
1999	IBM 5s 09	$1000	5%	$50
2000	IBM 10s 11	$1000	10%	$100
Year Sold				
2001	IBM 5s 99	$500	10% (Current Rate)	$50
2001	IBM 10s 11	$1000	10%	$100

Let's say you bought one IBM bond in 1999 and another in 2000. In 2001, you need the money for an emergency and want to sell the bonds. You could get $1000 for the 2000 bond because it pays the current interest rate. But you would get only about $500 for the bond you purchased in 1999. This is because, for an investor to make the current 10% yield on the 1999 bond, the investor would not pay more than $500 (10% of $500 is the $50 interest paid).

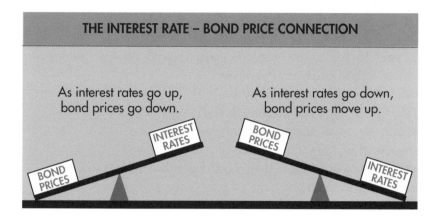

The 1999 bond goes down in price so that its interest rate matches the interest rate of the new bonds. The 1999 bond will still pay $1000 if you hold it until maturity. (If your bond were due to pay off in a year, the price would not go down much because the $1000 face value would be repaid soon.) The longer you have to wait for your $1000 principal, the more your old bond will fluctuate in value according to current interest rates.

> *The good news is that, if you buy a high-interest-rate bond and then interest rates go down, the value of your bond can go up temporarily. The point is that bonds have a great deal of "interest rate risk" if you need to sell them early.*

Risks from Interest Rate Changes

Standard advice to buyers of bonds is to "find out what is happening with the economy." Read about "key economic variables" such as inflation and economic growth. This allows you to *guess* which way interest rates are going. Then, if you think rates are going up, you might delay the purchase of bonds, or buy short-term Treasuries, so that your money would be available when rates are higher and you could invest at the higher rates. Similarly, if rates are going down, buy longer-term bonds so that you will lock in the higher rates for a longer period of time. And your bonds should go up in value in the meantime.

This all sounds very logical, but very few people can successfully predict interest rates consistently—not even professionals! Most economists aren't rich—and they would be if they could predict interest rate changes. You've probably heard the old insult, "If you laid all of the economists in the world end to end, they couldn't reach a conclusion."

I spend my whole day paying attention to various markets, but I would never base my investing, or my advice to you, solely on predicting interest rates. That would be foolhardy. That's another reason why I do a lot of my investing with the Chicken Stock strategy for long-term profits.

If you buy bonds, calculate the true return they will give you until maturity and *hold* them to maturity. Any other approach takes active, professional management, and is more risky.

This all probably seems somewhat confusing. The point is that bonds are *not* a simple, safe investment that you can put away and forget. And we haven't even covered the biggest risk associated with bonds!

DON'T OVERPAY FOR BONDS

You are at risk if you buy older bonds above face value in order to receive a higher rate of interest after rates have gone down. If you pay more than face value for a bond, you are *guaranteed to lose money* if you hold it until it matures, since it is worth only $1000 at that time. I prefer investments where you're almost guaranteed to *make* money, and I'm sure you do, too!

Inflation Risk

With all investments where your return is fixed, inflation can kill you. Even when inflation is low—say 3%—it means that the buying power of your $1000 has gone down when you get it back in 20 years. The $1000 you receive back will purchase not much more than half of what it could have when you loaned it 20 years earlier. You lose purchasing power every year. If your bond paid 6% and the inflation rate was 3%, your true return is only 3% a year. If you have to pay taxes on that money, your return will be even less. You're paying taxes on the full 6%, so if your combined tax bracket were 50% you'd earn nothing on your $1000 after taxes and inflation.

> Though the wages of the workman are commonly paid to him in money, his real revenue, like that of all other men, consists, not in money, but in the money's worth, not in the metal pieces, but in what can be got for them.
>
> —Adam Smith, 1776

Inflation risk is the biggest problem with fixed-rate investments like bonds. For instance, from the early 1920s to the late 1990s, there were 20 years when you would have lost money after accounting for inflation if you had invested in US government bonds. When your income is fixed for a long period of time, as with bonds, inflation chisels away at the value of your money.

As discussed in Chapters 1 and 3, inflation risk is the main reason why you need investments that will give you higher income every year. Stocks give you a "piece of the action" since good companies can raise their prices as inflation drives their costs up. They can also make more money by becoming more efficient. As you may recall from Chapter 3, Chicken Stocks give you higher income every year.

Credit Risk

The underlying risk of a bond can go up when a company's credit rating goes down. For instance, when Company A buys Company B for a high price, the new owner then has high debt. This makes the bonds in both companies less safe and they can go from top-rated triple-A bonds to junk bonds almost overnight.

Bankruptcy Risk

If a company fails and stops doing business, it goes bankrupt. While there are various forms of bankruptcy, in the extreme case (Chapter 7 bankruptcy), this means that the assets are sold off and the money used to pay debts.

In any form of bankruptcy, your investment is in danger. Some creditors have preference—bonds and other debts are paid off ahead of stockholders. So, if there are assets, you have a chance to receive part or all of your money back.

In a given year, as few as 1–5% of companies with bonds actually go bankrupt. In some of these cases, bondholders receive all of their money back, plus interest owed.

More likely to affect the value of your bond investment than bankruptcy itself is the *threat* of bankruptcy. For instance, years ago when Chrysler was reorganized, their bonds went down in value to a few hundred dollars because of the fear that the company might go bankrupt. In fact,

> There are two times in a man's life when he should not speculate: when he can't afford it, and when he can.
> —Mark Twain

when the government guaranteed Chrysler's loans, the company went on to great success under Lee Iacocca—and the bonds went back to their full $1000 value and were completely paid off. The government was also paid back early and made a profit from its loans.

Call Provision Risks

The companies that issue bonds often keep an extra edge for themselves, referred to as a *call provision*. This means that after the bonds have been out a certain number of years, often five or ten, the company can buy them back for face value or a little more.

Why would a company buy back their bonds early? Because, if interest rates go down, they can issue new bonds at a lower interest rate and use the money from the sale of the new bonds to buy back the older ones. This is similar to refinancing your house at a lower interest rate to save on monthly payments.

The money the company saves by buying back your bonds early is money you lose in interest income. If you buy a regular bond at 8% interest with a six-year term, you know you'll receive 8% interest for the next six years. With "callable" bonds, you cannot count on receiving the interest rate

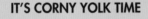

IT'S CORNY YOLK TIME

Cluck, cluck!

Have you heard about the new bonds that are being offered?

The *Politician Bonds* bear no interest.

The *Teenager Bonds* never reach maturity.

The *Benedict Arnold Bonds* have no principal.

for the full life of the bond. If interest rates go down, the company would buy back the bond and you wouldn't be able to buy another bond with a rate as high as your original bond. This is another factor that makes bonds not as safe as they look.

BOND RATINGS

Bond ratings are an estimate of the risk of your money not being paid back at maturity, as well as the risk of not getting your interest payments. Each bond is rated by various services like Moody's and Standard and Poor's. A "triple-A" (AAA) rated bond is considered very safe, an "A" less safe. A "B" is about the lowest rating used. So-called junk bonds are often not rated at all, or are rated so low as to be considered very risky. These ratings are conservative. Even most junk bonds pay off at maturity and do not go bankrupt. But odds of failure as low as 5% are considered high in the bond world.

These bond ratings can help you choose safer bonds. But high-rated bonds don't have to pay as much interest as low-

SOME SAMPLE LONG-TERM BOND RATINGS

 Here are just a few of the many different bond ratings by two of the companies that evaluate bonds. As you can see, different companies have different, though similar, ratings.

	MOODY'S	S&P
Prime, maximum safety	Aaa	AAA
High grade, high quality	Aa1	AA+
	Aa2	AA
	Aa3	AA-
Speculative	Ba2	BB
	Ba3	BB-
Highly Speculative	B1	B+
	B2	B
	B3	B-

"C"-rated bonds vary from "substantial risk to "may be in default." A bond rated "D" means the company is in default.

rated bonds, so you receive less interest when you buy safer bonds. This is another example of how it is hard to "beat the market" with bonds. The risk of each bond is already factored into the interest rate or price when you buy it.

BOND MUTUAL FUNDS

Be careful. Bond mutual funds can be dangerous!

When you think of buying bonds, it's natural to think of buying a bond mutual fund. This way, you get the advantages of mutual funds mentioned in Chapter 4 such as professional management and diversification. Unfortunately, many advisors also recommend this.

Regular mutual funds have serious drawbacks, but bond funds have even worse problems. I dislike bond funds as an investment vehicle for most people, for several reasons. You own a mutual fund, not bonds. Unlike individual bonds that can be held to maturity, a bond fund never matures. This means that the value of the fund varies directly with interest rates, subjecting you to tremendous ups and downs in the value of your principal in what was intended to be a "safe" investment. And, as mentioned in the opening example with the "Cohens," even your income can vary. Just as with stock mutual funds, you are also subject to the effects of other holders buying and selling the bond fund at the "wrong" times.

To repeat myself, you should *plan to hold a bond to maturity, when you get all your money back.* With a bond fund, you can't do that. You are simply speculating on interest rates!

USE A LADDERED PORTFOLIO TO MINIMIZE RISK

Two risks of having all your bond money in one type of bond can be avoided. The first risk is that, when your bonds mature, you'll get all your money back at once. Most people buy bonds for predictable interest income. Interest rates may have changed since you bought the bonds, so your interest payments can vary a lot over time. If you want to achieve stable interest payments from your bonds over a long period of time, there is a way to do it.

I recommend a *laddered portfolio* of individual bonds. A laddered portfolio means that the bonds have different maturity dates. When all your bonds expire at the same time and you want to reinvest the money in bonds, you are forced to accept the rate that is available at that time.

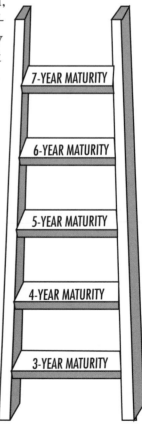

Since interest rates go up and down, by having bonds that expire at different times, you can more effectively receive the highest average interest rate available over a longer period. This makes your return more predictable over the long term.

"Ladders" Stabilize Your Interest

Typically, a ladder includes five steps. The most common ladder has bonds with maturity dates from 3 to 7 years. That's the average portfolio. Invest an equal amount of money at each maturity level. If you think interest rates are low, keep your maturity ladder shorter (for instance, 2-year, 3-year, 4-year, 5-year, and 6-year maturation dates). Then you'll receive your money sooner, so you can reinvest when rates are hopefully higher. If you think that interest rates are high, use a longer maturity ladder (4-year, 6-year, 8-year, 10-year, 12-year), to lock in the higher rate.

A laddered portfolio is normally a far better investment than a bond mutual fund. As already mentioned, bonds funds have no maturity date. With bond funds, you're constantly subjected to the ups and downs of interest rates. You're also whipsawed by the buying and selling of others. With bond funds, it takes years to recover when managers are forced to sell bonds when rates are high and bond prices are low

FOR THE DO-IT-YOURSELF INVESTOR

Some sources for bond research include *Barron's* weekly newspaper and, for online research, www.bondsonline.com and www.liquideffects.com. Both have a lot of information on bonds.

SUMMARY

In this chapter, I've discussed how to use bonds if you need more income now than stocks can provide. Many people don't understand the seesaw relationship between bonds and interest rates that puts you at great risk unless you hold bonds to maturity. You should avoid bond funds because their share price goes up and down with interest rates. To stabilize your income over many years, I've shown you how to "ladder" your bonds in a portfolio.

7

CONVERTIBLE BONDS
The Great American Premium Machine

Convertibles are appropriate for investors who want higher income than is available from common stock, together with greater appreciation potential than regular bonds offer.
—*BARRON'S FINANCE & INVESTMENT HANDBOOK*

IN ORDER TO MAKE BONDS FROM companies with less than A+ ratings more attractive to the investing public, or to get a lower interest rate, companies can add a "bonus." In addition to the normal pro–cedure of receiving your $1000 principal back when the bond matures, you can have the additional option of converting each bond to shares of the company stock. These are called *convertible bonds.*

If you pay $1000 for each bond, it might be convertible into 10 shares of stock valued at $50 each when the bonds are issued. In other words, the stock has to double for it to be worth the face value of the bond. However, this is not a bad deal. The bond may have a 15-year life and in that period many stocks will double, triple, or more.

VALUING CONVERTIBLE BONDS

Formulas for valuing investments are complex. Valued as a bond only, your convertible bond may pay a bit less interest than nonconvertible bonds of the same quality—say 8% instead of $8^1/5$%. The bond interest alone gives you some return on your capital and some safety. But for the small amount of interest that you are giving up, you also get the right to buy shares of stock—10 shares at $100 each in this case. These rights are sold separately and are called *warrants* or *options.* These are valuable. Your option in this case is worth more because it lasts for the life of the bond. Most traded stock options last a few months, or a year at the longest.

The exact value of your convertible bond isn't as important as the idea behind it. If the company stock goes down, you still receive your interest every year and your principal back upon maturity. If the stock goes up, you have a chance to receive more than your money back. The value of the conversion privilege will be reflected in the price of your bonds at all times, so you don't actually have to convert the bond to stock to make your profit.

CONVERTIBLE WEAKNESS

These convertible bonds are often issued by companies that are experiencing problems and would have to pay high rates of interest on regular bonds. Similarly, if they sold stock directly to raise money, they would probably have to sell shares for less than they are worth because of the problems. So in one way, convertible bonds are a sign of a company that has had problems. However, they can also be a sign of a company that expects things to get better and doesn't want to sell their stock at too cheap a price.

Because convertible bonds often originate from companies with problems, it is important to understand the current stability of the company that issues them. When I analyze companies offering convertible bonds, I look for a company with good prospects where the stock has a good chance of going up. Then, I analyze the income available to pay interest on the bonds for safety on the down side. If I've done my job right, I get a safe bond with a safe dividend that's higher than most stocks pay. And I receive an "equity kicker" in addition. That is, if I'm right and the stock goes up, I can receive a much higher return than based on the dividend alone because I can receive shares of stock at a reduced price.

CONVERTIBLES ARE MISUNDERSTOOD

Your average stock market wisdom is that a convertible bond is neither fish nor fowl. This means that, if you want income, you can buy a bond with higher payments. And, if you want stock appreciation, buying the regular stock of the same company will give you a higher return. Convertible bonds are a compromise—they are not as good as a pure bond in some ways and are not as good as a pure stock in other ways.

> We find that convertibles allow the investor...the benefits from both fixed-income and equity investments.
> —Scott L. Lummer & Mark W. Riepe, *Journal of Fixed Income*

This criticism is well and good IF you or I were a genius who could predict what interest rates and the stock market were going to do in the future for 5 to 10 years or more. Of course, I like to think I'm pretty knowledgeable about stocks and bonds since I spend my life with them. But nobody is good enough to know for certain what a particular stock and bond will do next year, let alone over a number of years! If some people could predict these things, they'd be using illegal information and be in jail, or be rich and not giving out advice!

Hey! There's nothing wrong with being a chicken!

CHICKEN POWER

Call me a "Chicken." I like to set up situations where, even if I'm wrong, my clients and I still make more money than average. That's what I like about convertible bonds. I can win two ways—with a better-than-average dividend (bond interest) OR with a stock that goes up. In fact, it's hard for a long-term investor to lose with this approach.

IT SLICES, IT DICES—WAIT, THERE'S MORE!

In addition to winning two ways by having a convertible bond that can act as a bond or a stock, I have another trick up my sleeve. Many stocks have active options traded on them. An option means that people own the right to buy the stock for a specific price for a limited time. For instance, people could buy an option to purchase "Widget" stock at a price of $5 anytime for six months. If they don't buy the stock, at the end of six months the option ends and has no value. By picking convertible bonds whose stocks have active options, you can increase your financial returns by a good percent.

Few investment advisors know that you can write *covered calls* (options) against these bonds. A covered call means you can sell the options without putting up any money, because you already own the stock. If you own a bond that is convertible into 10 shares of stock, you can sell others the right to buy 10 shares of that stock from you at a fixed price. This is because, if they exercised that option (decided they wanted the stock), you could convert your bond to the stock and sell the shares of stock at the option price. You could also buy the shares directly to re-

sell if that were cheaper for you, or buy an option yourself to cover the option you sold. The point is, the other person gets the shares and you could keep or convert the bonds.

Why would you want to sell options against your convertible bonds? Because you receive income from selling the options. This is in addition to your normal income from the interest payments on the bond. This increases your total return in almost complete safety.

An Example

Let's say you own a convertible bond that can be converted into 100 shares of Widget stock. When the bonds were first issued, the bond sold for $1000 and the stock sold for $5. So, if you converted then, your 100 shares of stock would be worth $500.

Now, let's say Widget stock is still at $5 a share. There could be options for the stock that allow the option holders to buy the stock at prices of $5, $7, and $10. The $5 option is valuable **because the stock is currently at that price,** so it might cost

$1 (depending on how long the option is good for). The option to buy the stock at $7 isn't worth as much because the stock would have to go up 40% to reach that price, so it might cost only $.25. And it would be even more of a long shot for the price to double and reach $10, so that option might only cost $.10. (I'm making up these numbers to show you how things work; I'm not trying to price them the way the market might.)

Because the convertible Widget bond gives you rights to 100 shares, you could sell options to purchase the stock at $7, good for 6 months, for $.25 per share. Normally, it would expire worthless because it's unlikely that the stock would rise from $5 to $7 in six month's time. You make another $50 a year income on each bond ($.25 per share times 100 shares that each bond is convertible into, twice a year). If your bond paid 5% interest a year ($50), with the

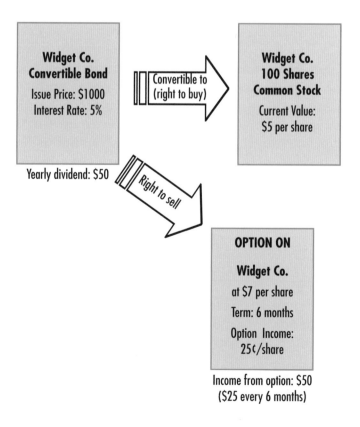

Widget Co.
Convertible Bond

Issue Price: $1000
Interest Rate: 5%

Convertible to
(right to buy)

Widget Co.
100 Shares
Common Stock

Current Value:
$5 per share

Yearly dividend: $50

Right to sell

OPTION ON

Widget Co.
at $7 per share
Term: 6 months
Option Income:
25¢/share

Income from option: $50
($25 every 6 months)

added option income, your
return would have doubled
to 10%! This is high. But
what if you only increased
the interest you received by
1%? That adds 20% to your
regular 5% interest pay-
ments. (You can double your
money in four years making
a return of 20%!)

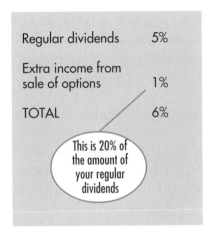

Regular dividends	5%
Extra income from sale of options	1%
TOTAL	6%

This is 20% of the amount of your regular dividends

Low Risk

Your risk in selling covered options is minimal. If the stock
goes up so high that the option buyer wants the shares,
you can either convert and deliver them, or buy out the
option and keep your bond. Done right, you increase your
income at minimal risk.

And the good thing is, you can keep doing this for as
long as you own the bond. There will continue to be new
options written at new prices forever. By picking the right
price and time, you can increase your income and keep the
bond forever. Of course, setting this up just right can be a
little complicated. I like to modestly think that this is one of
the many ways I earn my fees from clients as an advisor. I
select the type of bond that you'd want to write options on
and set up the system to reap long-term extra rewards. In
general, convertible bonds are hard to research for the do-
it-yourself investor.

SUMMARY

Convertible bonds have some of the advantages of
both bonds and stocks. You receive a fixed interest
rate and maturity date. You also receive the right to
convert your bonds into stock. This means, if the stock
goes up a lot, you make more money than you would from
the bond. I've also shown you how to increase your normal return by selling "call options" against your bonds.
Convertible preferred stocks are also mentioned.

8

SO YOU WANT A GUARANTEE
Annuities

---

*Every citizen will be able, in his productive years
when he is earning, to insure...[against] old age.*
—LYNDON B. JOHNSON

OF ALL THE INVESTMENTS YOU
hear discussed in the media, *variable
annuities* typically get the worst "rap." Most
"gurus" say you should just buy the underlying mutual funds and save money.
What they forget is the other benefits
annuities provide.

If you want a more conservative investment than bonds, with almost no risk,
annuities may fit the bill. Some of my clients call their annuity investments their

"Armageddon accounts." The money you place in annuities should be money you want to keep safe under all circumstances.

An annuity is a combination of insurance and investment. Just as an insurance policy guarantees a certain payment on your death, an annuity guarantees either a death benefit or the receipt of regular payments (*annuitization*) while you are alive.

ATTRACTIONS OF ANNUITIES
According to the *Barron's Finance & Investment Handbook*, annuities provide two basic attractions: • tax-deferred capital growth, and • the option of income for life or for a guaranteed period.

WHAT IS AN ANNUITY?

"Annuity" literally means a series of equal payments issued on a periodic schedule—annually, quarterly, or monthly. An annuity is a contract between you and an insurance company. Historically, a *fixed annuity* meant that you had made either a lump-sum payment or a series of payments into an annuity investment. In return, you would receive a fixed set of annuity payments if you lived and an insurance death benefit if you died. For instance, payments are often for the lifetime of the annuity recipient. These elements are specified in a *fixed annuity contract* that, in effect, is an insurance company's legally-binding promise to you.

A lot of complications surround annuities because there are hundreds of variations in the way they can be designed. There is also a lot of specialized language about them (which I won't go into here). The simple thing to remember is that annuities guarantee your investment return, just as insurance guarantees a return. When you buy them, however, you should plan to hold them at least seven years because annuities have stiff *surrender charges* if you withdraw funds within the first several years of entering a contract. There are also tax penalties if you withdraw money before age 59½.

Beware of early withdrawal penalties.

Variable Annuities

Variable annuities are annuities whose funds are placed in stocks and other variable-return instruments. They are designed to overcome the "fixed" rate of payments of regular annuities which may not keep up with inflation. There are many variations of these products.

Variable annuities are frequently available as so-called "qualified" retirement-plan options in employee benefit programs, permitting regular contributions into the accounts. There are lots of choices of how to invest the payments and how to receive the proceeds of an annuity contract. For instance, you can invest your annuity in mutual funds that are offered by the annuity.

Unlike fixed annuities, the performance of most variable annuity products is not predictable. That is, if their investments do not do well, you will not receive a good return. However, now some annuities provide a guaranteed minimum return, with a still-higher return, if the investments per-

form well. If you elect to receive regular payments (annuitize), you get whichever return
is higher, based on the guarantee or the
performance of the mutual funds. These are
good plans to look for.

BENEFITS OF ANNUITIES

Tax-Free Growth

Annuity investment earnings are exempt
from all taxation while they remain in the
contract. Regular (annuitized) disbursements are subject to taxes, but do not influ-
ence your Social Security entitlements.
When you receive annuity payments, the IRS
normally considers the payments to be a
combination of earnings and of your original investment (the principal) in the annuity. The original investment is generally not
taxed because it's considered a return of
principal.

Easy to Pass On

If you die with all your money still in the
annuity, your annuity contract can be
passed on to your beneficiary without
getting tied up in your will (probate). Your
beneficiary will usually be required to withdraw the money within a year and pay any
appropriate taxes. If you've begun to draw
regular payments, what happens upon your
death depends on your contract.

Unlimited Contributions

Unlike other retirement-related plans, there
generally are no limits on the amount of
money you may invest in annuity contracts.
If you don't have much in IRAs or 401(k)s

> Variable annuities
> have been the
> fastest-selling
> investment
> product since
> 1995.
> —*Barron's Investing
> for Retirement*

and want to put more than the limits allow into your retirement accounts, annuities have no limits. You can put $100,000 a year—or any other amount—into annuities.

Benefits Increase with Market Increases

Many annuity contracts increase the amount of your guaranteed principal after a set time, usually every year; this is known as a step-up provision. Even better, once it is increased, it never goes down again, even if your investments crash. *This means that you benefit from market increases, but don't lose if it goes down.*

Flexible Payouts

You may decide to receive your payments from an annuity contract in a variety of ways, the most common being guaranteed periodic payments (usually monthly) for as long as you and, usually, your beneficiary, may live. Many retirement plan programs recommend what's called "period certain" annuitization plans. These plans offer periodic payments for a guaranteed minimum number of years, or your remaining life span, whichever is greater. If you had a period certain annuity with a 10-year guarantee, and you died after the first year, your beneficiaries would receive nine additional years of payments. If you lived 30 more years, you'd get 30 years of additional payments.

A NO-TAX SWITCH

If you want to switch one annuity for another, you can do so without paying taxes. This allows you to take advantage of enhanced features of newer annuities. Exchanging one contract for another is known as a *1035 exchange* (named after Section 1035 of the federal tax code). In contrast, if you switch from one mutual fund to another, it's a "taxable event."

Variety of Investments

Variable annuities give you a wide selection of investment fund products in which to place your annuity investments. These investment funds look and act a lot like mutual funds. While the annual fees for running variable annuity accounts are higher than for mutual funds alone, there generally are no up-front fees, meaning all of your investment is working for you right away.

DRAWBACKS TO ANNUITIES

Higher Fees

As already mentioned, the fees on annuities are usually higher than on mutual funds. Based on Lipper Analytic Service data, the average investment management expenses for variable annuities were actually lower than for the average mutual fund. Unfortunately, variable annuities had another insurance expense that raised their average annual charge to 2.03%, which was .65% higher than the average mutual fund charge of 1.38%.

Early Withdrawal Penalties

Remember, if you pull money out of annuities early, particularly in the first seven

---

HOW SAFE IS THE INSURANCE?

Annuities give you an extra layer of insurance for your investments. But, what if your insurance company goes bankrupt? It happened years ago with an annuity issuer called Baldwin United. In that case, annuity holders were paid in full by the company assets plus another insurance fund. Insurance companies have a "fall back" fund that is used in this kind of rare case.

Another thing worth mentioning is that Baldwin United wasn't much of an insurance company. They were the Baldwin piano company that got into insurance without much knowledge. So, another conservative rule is don't buy your insurance from a piano company!

years, you pay surrender charges from the annuity issuers. This is because they deferred sales charges when you bought the annuity. Depending on your age or time in a plan, there can be a 10% IRS penalty on early withdrawals, just as for many other retirement plans.

Taxable Gains

When you take money out of annuities, the gains on your investment (not your contributions) are taxed as ordinary income. Depending on what tax bracket you are in, and the capital gains tax rate, you may pay more taxes on these gains than in a mutual fund. And if you die, your heirs pay taxes on the gains in your annuity. With mutual funds, their cost basis is "stepped-up." This means that their cost is considered to be the value when they inherit, so they would save taxes down the road when they sell.

WHO SHOULD BUY ANNUITIES?

As I said at the beginning of this chapter, you might buy an annuity when you want extra guarantees and safety for your returns. When you buy a variable annuity with a guaranteed minimum return, in some ways, you can "have your cake and eat it, too." If your chosen investments go up, you make more money. If they don't, you still get the guaranteed return.

The ideal annuity buyer is 52 or older. Annuities are less attractive to younger investors because there is a 10% tax penalty if you withdraw money from your annuity before age 59½ for reasons other than death or disability. The ideal annuity buyers have already contributed the maximum amount to their existing tax-deferred retirement plans, such as a 401(k), 403(b), or IRA. That's because you are already building up tax-deferred money in those plans, and those savings vehicles cost less than an annuity.

Unlike many retirement accounts, you can put as much money as you want into an annuity and there is no penalty for keeping money in an annuity contract past the age of 70½ (assuming, of course, that it's not part of a retirement program). You, the annuity owner, determine when the funds come out of the account, and in what form.

SUMMARY

I prefer the Chicken Stock strategy (Chapter 3) to annuities over the long term. Annuities are for those who are *really* afraid of the stock market. They give you an extra layer of guarantee, for which you pay a price. They can be a good way to get a lot of money into a retirement plan in a hurry. They are not the ideal way to pass money to others, unless your estate is below the taxable limit.

If you decide you want the guarantee of an annuity, here are some things to consider:

- Look for a variable annuity with a guaranteed minimum return. This gives you the advantages of both fixed and variable plans.
- Plan on avoiding any withdrawals for at least seven years. On most annuities, you will pay hefty surrender fees if you pull out during the first seven to eight years of your contract.
- Examine the fee structure and details of a contract carefully. Fees and variations of programs differ by company and by contract, so make sure you are comfortable that you are getting good value for what you are paying.
- Check the credit rating of the insurance company issuing the annuity.

9

YOUR HIRED HELP
Do You Really Need Stockbrokers and Financial Consultants?

It has been a problem since the dawn of the retail brokerage business: Brokers have a strong incentive to get customers to trade when it might be in clients' interests to do nothing.
—BUSINESS WEEK, JULY 14, 1997

THESE DAYS, THERE ARE A LOT of people out there who call themselves *financial consultants.* That's now the preferred title for people who used to specialize in selling insurance. There are many others who have some financial expertise, from your banker and trust officer to your family lawyer and accountant. There are fee-based financial planners. There are even psychic money consultants!

Unfortunately, many advisors act like they're doing you a favor to take your money. Don't be fooled—they work for you. They're your "hired help." They need to meet your needs and you should be in control.

MY FINANCIAL ADVICE PHILOSOPHY

Depending on your needs, some of the types of advisors mentioned above may be of help to you. It really depends on what your investments are—you want an expert in your type of investment.

"Prescription without diagnosis is malpractice" started as a saying about physicians, but applies to all advice givers. I like the doctor analogy. If you have a foot problem, you go to a podiatrist, not a gynecologist. If you have a skin problem, you go to a dermatologist, not a cardiologist. It's the same when it comes to your financial health.

If you believe—as I do—that owning a "piece of America" is a great long-term strategy, it seems to me that a licensed stockbroker would be your financial advisor of choice for stocks and bonds. It is a big job just to keep up on the stock market. I don't have the time—or the knowledge—to sell the right insurance coverage for a particular individual (despite the fact that I'm

> We subscribe to Fred's investing philosophy. Even though we retired to a different city, the trust generated by Fred kept us investing our retirement funds with him."
>
> —Rollie and Sondra Ferris, clients

licensed to do so). It's a full-time job just to follow the stock and bond markets. When our clients need this type of advice, I always refer them to a specialist.

WHAT IS A STOCKBROKER?

Most stockbrokers are now called financial advisors or consultants because they should do more than just buy and sell stocks. Unfortunately, the term stockbroker came to imply a "salesperson" whose main goal was to get you to buy and sell more frequently to generate commissions.

Before I help people invest in stocks or bonds, I always do an overall financial analysis, to make sure the stock or bond investment is appropriate for their particular needs.

Costs versus Services

Many types of advisors can now "execute orders" for stocks and bonds. If you already know what you want to buy or sell, you can trade online yourself for almost no transaction fee. And many other companies can handle the transaction for you for varying fees.

I'm old fashioned. I grew up in those "ancient times" when stockbrokers provided full-service advice for investors. They got paid for good advice and investment research. Customers paid full-service commissions and the best brokers were worth far more than the commissions they received.

Good advice is cheap, no matter how much it costs!

My goal for many years has been to work for people who want to be long-term investors. I spend my time working for clients, to help them obtain the best stock or bond investments for their needs. I want to be a bargain for what I deliver, provide top value, and deliver enough to be well-compensated for my efforts.

FOOLS, FRAUDS, AND OTHER SO-CALLED EXPERTS

Before I go on, I'd like to briefly discuss "popular" experts who you might see in bookstores or in the media. My general message is BE CAREFUL. Some of these so-called "experts" are incompetent, or worse.

There Are "Experts" and Experts

Before I talk about the fools and frauds, I should also say that there are some very reputable and helpful popular experts. Louis Rukeyser is probably best known for his *Wall Street Week* television show. His background was not investing; he was a political and foreign news correspondent. When he returned to New York from overseas, he pioneered the position of economic correspondent and commentator. A couple of years later, *Wall Street Week* went on the air. No other show was so entertaining and accessible for the average investor.

Over the years, Rukeyser surrounded himself with experts on his panel and interviewed hundreds more. While he may not always be right, he's honest, clear—and still entertaining.

Jane Bryant Quinn, author of a national financial newspaper column and books, is another expert who seems to have the best interests of her readers at heart. She appears to be particularly concerned about "insiders" taking advantage of "average" people. I don't know either of these people personally, so I am offering them only as examples of popular experts who look good, based on what I do know.

> There's a lot of bad advice out there. The majority of [financial] planners are delivery systems for prepackaged financial products...Most planners have to sell or starve.
>
> —Jane Bryant Quinn, *Making the Most of Your Money*

Why Dangerous Advice Survives

There are two general reasons why there are popular advisors out there who can be dangerous to your financial health. The first reason is somewhat abstract; the second is obvious.

1 Some advisors are always going to be accurate by pure chance. If you flip a coin ten times, on average, it will come up heads five times and tails five times. Statisticians can tell you how many times a coin is expected to come up heads exactly half the time out of 100 tries and how many times it won't. It's called a *normal distribution.* This means that, *totally by chance,* a few times you could flip a coin ten times and it would come up all heads or all tails.

STOCK SELECTION BY DARTS

It's impossible to reliably predict the stock market over the short term. *The Wall Street Journal* occasionally runs a contest between investment professionals and dart board selections (WSJ employees throw darts at stock tables tacked to a wall).

Since the contest began in 1990, the investment professionals have beaten the dart board about 60% of the time. That's not much better than chance.

Chance Adds Up

In the financial advisor world, there are far more than 100 people giving advice. There are probably tens of thousands, if not more. By pure chance, a few of them are going to be right at any one time. The few who are right, naturally think it is not by luck. But, most of the time, it is. They may do great one year because of specific market conditions, but very seldom will they beat the market the next year, or for many years in a row as my Chicken Stock strategy has.

If someone uses a strategy and makes a lot of money, it's natural to write a book about it, or sell newsletters or seminars. Under specific market conditions, the strategy may work for a year or two. But it is just random chance most of the time. I remember a famous book years ago by Nicholas Darvas, *How I Made $2,000,000 in the Stock Market.* As I recall, Darvas was a dancer, and as he toured around the world he bought stocks if they went up a certain amount, sold if they went down, bought them back as they started up again, and so forth.

This kind of technical strategy can work for a while under certain conditions, and it worked for him. Unfortunately, it did not work for most of the people who bought the book because conditions had changed. Another problem with most "strategies" is that as other people become aware of them and use them, this, in itself, changes the conditions so that the strategy no longer works.

Adopting the strategy of whoever has done the best in the last year is almost a sure way to lose money in the long run. This was also mentioned in the mutual funds chapter. The fund that does best one year very seldom does best the next. As I said, this is just the laws of chance at work.

2 The second reason to be cautious about "popular" advisors is because they can make a lot of money by exaggerating their successes. If you think they are great, they can sell you newsletters, courses, "inner circle" memberships, and so forth. This makes them a lot of money.

Two examples that are well known, are Wade Cook's and Charles Givens' programs. As described in *Forbes* magazine, Wade Cook first made money in the real estate area recommending that you buy and sell mortgages (*The Real Estate Money Machine*). In 1984, he filed for bankruptcy. Instead of disappearing, he came back with the *Wall Street Money Machine* and other bestselling books. His three-day workshops were priced at $4,700. He took his company public and the stock went up 500%.

The big problem is that Cook promises "safe 20% monthly returns," double your money every 2 to 4$\frac{1}{2}$

months, and so forth. (While it is always possible after the fact to find a strategy that would have performed well, few find them ahead of time.) Talking about these exaggerated claims for Cook's seminars, Phil Feigin, a securities commissioner for the state of Colorado, said, "In my 17 years experience, any claim promising or projecting 300% returns has been proven not only to be false but fraudulent." Think about it with your own common sense for a minute. If it sounds too good to be true, it usually is. If the market is charging up, it may be possible to make easy money for a while, but eventually it always corrects down from this kind of excess.

According to *Forbes* magazine, Cook's company was the subject of a fraud investigation by the SEC starting in March, 1996. Naturally, he denied any wrongdoing and kept right on selling his system. Mark Skousen, a financial writer, summed it up this way, "This is the same nonsense Cook was peddling nearly 20 years ago, but this time it's stocks, not real estate. The advice is just as dangerous and the people buying it are just as uninformed."

MODERN-DAY SNAKE OIL SALESPEOPLE

We tend to laugh at images of people being taken in by the salesman hawking his patent medicine. Even today, however, with our access to millions of sources of information, we are no less immune to being swayed by silver-tongued salespeople (commercials, authors, seminar-givers, and so forth).

Even when there is no evidence that a particular diet concoction or stock investment program works, thousands of us fall for the patter.

Are we optimists or fools? Probably some of both. We're optimistic in that we'd like to believe there is a quick and easy fix for our problems. And most of us want to trust people. But we're foolish if we don't take a skeptical view of any promise of quick and easy results.

Another self-styled investment guru is Charles Givens. With book titles like *Wealth Without Risk,* his appeal and implausibility is immediately evident. There is always risk when money is involved.

For $2000 you could buy a membership in his organization. His advice tended to be simplistic, dogmatic, and occasionally contradictory, according to *The Wall Street Journal* and others. There have been successful lawsuits against him, as well as criminal convictions.

More Overstated Claims

An example of a more subtle problem is presented by those who are well-intentioned. Often they have achieved personal success and then write a book to sell their ideas to others. For instance, one author of a bestselling book has been on *Oprah* many times as well as other network TV shows. *Forbes* magazine published a thorough discussion of the exaggerations of this author's credentials (which the author then corrected in subsequent editions of the book). "Everything you need to know to provide for yourself and your family," the book jacket proclaims—and you get such tips as: 'Use self-service gas pumps rather than full-serve.' Or, 'Use coins, not your calling card, in pay phones.' On a recent *Oprah,* this advisor suggested that viewers search through their closets for misplaced money." Not exactly investment advice!

Even the investment returns for the Beardstown Ladies (a group of older women who started an investment club, and later

> **Most liars can fool most people most of the time.**
> —Paul Ekman, psychologist (on research showing people to be surprisingly inept at detecting lies)

wrote several books) were originally exaggerated. I'm sure they were well-intentioned, but this doesn't help people trying to succeed in the complex task of investing.

The following sections suggest what to look for in a serious financial advisor.

8 TIPS FOR SELECTING YOUR FINANCIAL ADVISORS

The selection of good advisors may be the most important thing you can do to ensure your financial health. While any insurance agent can sell you business or home insurance, the best ones will make sure that you get the protection that you actually need to protect your lifestyle. The same is true for my area. Many places can execute an order for you. But getting good advice on what stocks to buy is a different issue.

1 **DO YOUR HOMEWORK.** Perhaps the best way to find good financial advisors is to evaluate their personalities and investment philosophies in person. A good way to do this is to meet them when they are speaking on the topic of investments. There are limitations to meeting someone in person and making a judgment about their professional competence. But it allows you to get a feel for their style and decide whether you'd enjoy working with them. You can also ask questions about their investment philosophies, to make sure that they fit your needs.

To give myself and others who have written investment books a "plug," I'd like to add that reading an article or book by an investment advisor can *often* tell you more than simply meeting them in person, particularly if your meeting is at a social occasion where there is little time for serious conversation. Written material allows you to understand an advisor's approach in depth and to think about it at your own pace. While many top advisors will not work with people unless their accounts are over $1 million, I enjoy hearing from readers, viewers, and listeners, and often can be of help.

2 **DO NOT TAKE REFERRALS FROM OTHERS AT FACE VALUE.** The most common advice given in other books about how to find financial advisors is to ask for referrals from friends and experts such as your banker, accountant, and so forth. Unfortunately, there have been a number of documented cases when the most popular stockbrokers in town whose clients were all the "right people" were actually losing money for their clients. These brokers had good social skills at the "country club," but not good investment skills.

Many brokers push only what their firm tells them to. Sometimes these investments *du jour* are those where the firm makes the most money or that pay the highest commissions, rather than what is best for the client. This can be seen in the frequent preference for selling new mutual funds (that happen to pay high commissions) rather than older funds with long-established performance records and lower commissions.

> Bulls and bears aren't responsible for as many stock losses as bum steers.
>
> —Olin Miller

If you obtain multiple referrals from others, this will give you a pool of people as potential advisors. But don't rely on the opinions of others. Make sure you find out if your candidates share your investment philosophy. Only then can they help you accomplish *your* objectives.

3 **INTERVIEW ANY ADVISOR WITH WHOM YOU ARE INTERESTED IN WORKING.** Many financial experts suggest that you interview possible brokers or other investment advisors. However, they generally make few suggestions about how to actually go about it. Start by summarizing your own investment experience and the size of your accounts. You can do this in an initial conversation on the phone. The prospective advisor may decline your account at this early point (usually if your account is small). If not, set up a time when you can talk in greater depth.

Most people advise that you interview each candidate in person. If this makes you feel comfortable, that's fine, but it is inefficient. Most people end up doing all their business by phone. Their advisor calls them or they call their advisor, depending on the circumstances. You can save a lot of time by doing your preliminary screening of advisors on the phone.

RATE POTENTIAL ADVISORS ON...

✓ Investment philosophy

✓ Accessibility

✓ Personal investments

✓ Length of time advising

✓ Investment recommendations personalized, not generic

✓ Client recommendations

✓ Fees

In trying to reach them by phone, you'll learn another item: how accessible they are. If you can't get the information you need, these advisors may not be available when you need them later. At this point, remember: If they don't make time for you now while they're trying *to get* your business, they'll be even less likely to make time for you when you're a client. Similarly, if you don't like their manner on the phone, you can rule them out early. In my case, because I spend a great amount of time managing clients' investments, my partner generally handles the first meeting and I come in later.

Ask potential advisors how they invest their own money. If they're not in the stock market, rule them out immediately, unless they explain that they think the market is about to crash. If they're not in the market personally, they must not be making much money or are not serious about the market. In either case, try someone else.

Find out how long they've been a broker. If they haven't been a broker through at least one major downturn, they won't be seasoned enough to provide mature advice for you. The best case would be if they've been through the crash of 1987. This was a severe enough crash that, having lived through it, they won't assume that the market always goes up, as many less-experienced brokers do. Brokers who have been in the business for years also do not have to spend their time recruiting new clients. For their first few years, most new brokers make hundreds of cold calls to strangers every day to pick up new accounts, or they don't stay in the business. So, if you get a new broker, they won't have time to do research on stocks, or they may be "flunking out" as a broker and not be around much longer to help you.

This is important!

4 **ASK THIS "TRICK" QUES-TION.** A good question to start with is "What would you recommend for me at this point in time?" *This is a trick question!* If all they know is your investment experience and the size of your account, they should NOT make any recommendations. If they do so without asking you further questions to determine

Remember: Prescription without diagnosis is malpractice.

your investment goals, then they are just fitting you into a general model that they push on all their clients.

If they ask about your investment goals, how much time until you plan to retire, your need for money now and later, and so forth, then your candidates are still in the running. They should bring up a discussion of your investment philosophy and share theirs with you. If they don't, you should ask them about their philosophy and approach.

5 **FIND OUT WHAT OTHER CLIENTS SAY.** The last major thing you might want to do to check up on your prospective advisor (your "due diligence") is to ask for client referrals. While brokers may be reluctant to give out client names, they should have a few favorites who would be happy to talk with you about how the advisor is to work with. If they refuse to give referral sources, you should probably rule them out.

When you talk to the advisor's customers, ask them:

- what types of investments they make
- how they've performed compared to the market
- how easy the advisor is to reach
- does the broker call pushing investments that his or her company supports that don't relate to the client's investment goals.
- what they think the broker's investment philosophy is. If different clients give radically different answers, then the broker may not have a real philosophy: he or she may simply be telling each client what the client wants to hear.

These questions should help you chose the broker you want to work with, or narrow the field considerably.

6 **MAKE A PERSONAL VISIT.** If you like to deal with people directly, now is the time for a personal visit. Even if the advisor offers to come to your home or office, you'll learn more by visiting his or her office.

If you're interested in reading research reports and other resources, check out what's available. If the advisor's office is more convenient than your local library, or has a better collection than the library, you may want to visit occasionally, to read expensive newsletters or research summaries like *Value Line*. (Brokers will also sometimes send you copies of parts that affect you.)

You'll remember that I also mentioned that newer brokers have to spend all their time on the phone looking for new clients. Visiting your potential broker will give you an idea if that is what the brokers in this office do. If they all are making calls most of the time, they may be better salespeople than financial advisors.

DO YOU NEED A HANG OUT?

In the "old days," some people liked to "hang out" at their broker's office. Some still do. If this could be you, you'll want to see what it is like and if they have a place for visitors to sit and watch the "ticker tape." (Today this is usually an electronic display with prices on stocks and brief summaries of news that might affect stock prices).

7 COMPARE FEES. If you still have more than one advisor in consideration after these steps, you have more choices than most people. If you can't decide between two brokers, look at their fees. The odds are that the costs of two brokers who are this well qualified will be similar. But, if there is a difference, that can be your deciding point.

8 START WITH A "TEST" ACCOUNT OR ACCOUNTS. If I found two advisors whom I liked who shared my investment philosophy, I would be tempted to open test accounts with both of them. Unfortunately, many times brokers will be all sweetness and light until they get your money invested. Then they practically ignore you. Their attitude is that of an old-fashioned salesperson—once they have your money, they move on. Professional financial advisors are more sincere about building the relationship and will be just as helpful after they have your money. Unfortunately, if they are very smooth, often the only way to determine how they will service your account is after they have your money. (Unless, of course, you interviewed some of the broker's clients—then you may have found this out.)

Don't put all of your eggs in one basket!

WHAT REAL PEOPLE DO

The way I've suggested that you screen for an advisor is both simpler than what most others recommend, and more complicated than most investors will go through.

In most cases, people use the only advisor they know. Hopefully, if you can't take the time to carefully screen your broker, you'll apply at least the last point I mentioned. Start with a test account. Don't turn over everything you have to invest in a hurry. This will help you get to know your financial advisor and decide if you should continue to look for a better one.

HOW I WORK WITH CLIENTS

What I've described as the general ways to select and work with financial advisors are actually a bit different than the way my clients and I like to work together. Typically, after some preliminary contacts, we sit down and determine the clients' needs for income now and later, willingness to take risks, and so forth. I then create a written proposal with projections showing where I think they should be in a few years. Most people then hire me to manage their portfolio.

I use a limited power of attorney to handle their transactions. I receive a fee based on their assets, but no commissions from buying and selling their holdings. The only way I make more money is if their portfolio goes up in value.

My typical client has the majority of their holdings in Chicken Stocks (see Chapter 3) and perhaps some assets in bonds or more aggressive investments. They don't really want to discuss the details of every move I make. They want me to take care of it and send them a certain amount of income. We provide monthly statements. Unlike most advisors for individuals, we also provide quarterly performance reports. We show changes since they started with us, for the last year, and for the last quarter. This way, my clients always know how their money is performing. (See Chapter 12 for sample client portfolios.)

CLIENT-CENTERED FINANCIAL ADVISING

- ✓ Needs assessment
- ✓ Risk tolerance assessment
- ✓ No commissions paid on buying and selling holdings; fee-based
- ✓ Monthly statements
- ✓ Quarterly performance reports

5 PROBLEMS WITH BROKERAGE HOUSE RESEARCH

In the process of choosing a financial advisor, you should define what you want from the relationship. You will at least want them to have established criteria about stocks that would make good investments. While you don't hire advisors for their research ability, they should have enough interest in the stocks they recommend to do *some* research. Full-service advisors have research departments to do the heavy research. Unfortunately, there are several problems with this:

1 **THEY'RE DOING RESEARCH FOR THE "AVERAGE" CLIENT.** Your needs are not average. You need a broker who tailors recommendations for your specific situation.

2 **STOCKBROKERAGE RESEARCH TENDS TO "RUN WITH THE PACK."** That is, big companies make presentations to analysts and make the case why their stock should be bought. Most of the analysts represent giant accounts that buy millions of dollars of stock at a time. Only the bigger companies can afford to make these presentations and get analysts' attention. These huge companies are fine for large institutional investors like pension funds and insurance companies. But, if you buy stocks like these, you are always going to know less than these big investors.

When a company makes a presentation about their stock to analysts from many brokerage houses, and the analysts are impressed with it and recommend it, the stock often immediately goes up substantially. This makes you a mouse in the middle of elephants—without the cartoon ability to scare the elephants. You may not get trampled, but you won't have a comfortable time!

3 **A VARIATION OF "GRADE INFLA-TION" OCCURS WITH ANALYSTS' RATINGS OF STOCKS.** Most brokerage ratings of stocks vary from "strong buy" to "hold," with few recommendations for outright sells. This means that a "buy" doesn't mean much, and a "hold" usually means sell. It is well known by insiders that brokerage analysts don't like to criticize stocks because they have conflicts of interest. Their brokerage may, at some point in the future, be competing to sell new stock or bonds for the company being analyzed. If the analysts criticize the stock, the big companies may hold it against the brokerage firms.

REPORT CARD	
Stock A	A
Stock B	A+
Stock C	A
Stock D	B+
Stock E	A+

4 **IF BIG BROKERAGES ARE RECOMMENDING A STOCK, YOU CAN BE SURE THAT OTHERS HAVE ALREADY BOUGHT THE STOCK AND THUS DRIVEN UP THE PRICE.** In the past, companies often made presentations of new information to big buyers first. Since this put the smaller investor at a disadvantage, there are now rules that this information must be more widely disseminated (through the Internet and other mechanisms). But, human nature being what it is, there will always be people who get the information ahead of time. The people with the information make more money than the people without. (If you follow my philosophy of being a long-term investor in strong companies, this won't hurt you in the long run.)

5 **IF AN ADVISOR ONLY GIVES YOU INFORMATION FROM HIS OR HER**

OWN RESEARCH DEPARTMENT, YOUR ADVISOR ISN'T TAKING AN ACTIVE INTEREST IN THE MARKET. Advisors who follow the stock market will naturally develop their own pet theories and stocks. Brokers have access to lots of information, including what their successful clients are doing. If they're not using this information and passing it on to you, they're not going to help educate you and bring you ideas.

The best cases are when advisors recommend several stocks that fit your criteria that their firm is not pushing. The advisor can then provide you with more objective information about the stocks from *Value Line* or *Standard and Poor's* reports. They should also be able to briefly and clearly explain why they like the stock.

> If a broker can't explain his or her philosophy briefly and clearly, the broker probably doesn't have one.

This brings up a related point that is central to your relationship with your advisor: If they can't explain why they like a stock in 20 words or less, they are probably just parroting some analyst's report.

WHAT DOES "FULL SERVICE" MEAN?

Discount brokers only place your buy and sell orders, so you need to do all of your own research and make all the decisions yourself. In this case, you might as well deal with the least expensive brokers online who never talk with you. (But note: In the chapter about online investing you'll learn that the "low cost" commission may cost you a lot in execution costs, so the lowest-priced broker may actually be more expensive than other brokers.)

Nowadays, there are several variations of "service" besides "full service." Full-service brokers are supposed to give you advice and guidance about your possible investments. They should bring you ideas, and offer money market accounts that pay far more than the bank and are very flexible. They should have in-house research reports and send you material from other sources as well. They should keep up on breaking news about the stocks they recommend and notify you if there is something you need to act on.

Discount brokers are now providing a number of partial service options. For an extra fee they may offer you opinions, or some research. If these variations are important to you, ask your broker candidates how much service they provide.

> *I recommend that you use a full-service broker. I may be biased, but if you're investing long-term, as I recommend, the extra cost should be nothing compared to your extra profits over the years. A full-service broker can give you advice and help you with your broader financial concerns.*

IT'S CORNY YOLK TIME

Cluck, cluck!

The Waltons invited their new neighbors, the Spits, over to dinner. During dinner, Mr. Spit asked Mr. Walton what he did for a living.

Four-year-old Brian Walton jumped in and said "Daddy is a fisherman!"

Mrs. Walton replied, "Brian, why do you say that? Your daddy is a stockbroker, not a fisherman."

"But, Mom, every time we visit Dad at work and he hangs up the phone, he laughs, rubs his hands together, and says, ' I just caught another fish.'"

WHAT DO YOU WANT FROM A BROKER/ADVISOR?

In Chapter 1, you answered some questions about your own attitudes toward risk and how long you expected to hold stocks. In order to tell if an advisor is a good fit for you, you need to know your needs as an investor and what you want from a broker.

The first thing anyone needs from a stockbroker is a sense of comfort. If the broker reminds you of the untrustworthy Eddie Haskell on *Leave It to Beaver,* or a used car salesman, you won't be comfortable. If a broker seems trustworthy, there are a number of other characteristics that you probably want him or her to have:

- an investment philosophy you agree with
- friendliness
- ability and willingness to educate you about investments
- a good track record
- ability to explain your investments to your lawyer, accountant or other advisors
- ability to work well with other people on your financial team

You may want all of the above from an advisor, or only some of it. This is just a list to stimulate your thinking. As long as there is trust and good communication between you and your broker, things should work out well.

One other point may be worth mentioning. Sometimes people spend so much time analyzing issues such as choosing an advisor, that they forget the point of the exercise. That point is to make the best decision you can with the information you have and *get started.* If you don't act to improve your investments, you are making a decision to allow inflation to gradually eat your assets away. No advisor is perfect—not even me! If you can find a good one you're comfortable with, you'll be able to enjoy the investing experience while building your assets.

SUMMARY

The best way to find a stockbroker or other investment advisor is to get to know them in a way that
lets you understand their investment philosophy.
Going to seminars or reading what they've written is ideal.
Other ways to screen and select a broker are discussed.
The main objective is to find someone who is competent
and who uses an investment approach you are comfortable with. You should also be comfortable with the person
and be sure that they have your best interests at heart,
not their commissions!

10

THE WORLD OF ONLINE INVESTING
Caveats a'Plenty

The most important piece of advice is to do your homework and get the facts on any investment you learn about on the Web.
—NANCY SMITH, SECURITIES AND EXCHANGE COMMISSION

NO MODERN INVESTMENT BOOK would be complete these days without some discussion of online investing. To summarize this chapter, the good things about the online investing world are that the cost of stock transactions is much lower online and there is a lot of information available. The bad thing about online investing is that there is a lot of distracting and even deliberately misleading information online that is used to manipulate stock prices. I am more cautious than most about online information. However, after I elaborate the pros and cons, I will start you out with some resources online that will lead you to as many more as you have the patience for.

WHAT IS "ONLINE" INVESTING?

To start with the basics, online investing simply refers to the use of the Internet for purchasing stocks and other investments, or doing research on them. You probably already know that the Internet is a way of connecting computers all over the world. This is also called the World Wide Web and the Information Superhighway.

By connecting millions of computers at almost no expense, the cost of exchanging, and publishing, information has gone way down. For this reason, and the possibility of attracting new business, millions of companies and individuals have created Web sites that are open to anyone. For instance, many stock brokerage firms, investment newsletters, and others have put up information about investing that you can read or print out for free. There are also many "chat rooms" and "message boards" where people "talk" about stocks.

THE BENEFITS OF ONLINE INVESTING

There are several potential benefits of using online resources to invest or do investment research. The two main ones are:
- lower transaction costs
- more information available

Other benefits of online investing are somewhat more subtle, or are included in the two main reasons above. For instance, the ability of millions of people to exchange information not only makes more information available, but is a force for democratization—involving everyone on a more equal basis.

This is not just a philosophical issue. It has practical ramifications. For example, in the "old days" before 2000, companies would often provide information to analysts and the large mutual funds before they released it to the public. This practice really did help the "rich get richer."

These big players are the most important buyers of company stocks and bonds. Giving them information early helped them make more money or protect their positions—as well as feel special. Of course, it also hurt the "little guys."

The excuse for only including a few people in early or specialized announcements was that it was impractical to tell everyone. The Internet, however, made such announcements easy to make to anyone who wanted to listen. Thus, the full disclosure rule was adopted by the SEC to help the average investor.

USE THE INTERNET FOR RESEARCH

There are Web sites that give information on analysts and so forth. For updates, see my Web site: thesiegelgroup.com.

Networking with Other Investors

Another aspect of online investing is the many "chat rooms" available. These are places online where people can "talk" with each other by sending messages that are read instantly by the rest of the group. With chat groups, if anyone knows something, more people can be told more quickly than in days past when that person would be sharing the information in person or via the telephone. Your circle is also expanded because you don't have to know any of the people in the online group. This theoretically further improves the flow of information.

Information is key in making good investment decisions. It also educates people. For example, if you want to know more about a computer stock, most groups include people who actually work for computer companies who will share information.

An Information Gold Mine

On a more concrete note, you can do lots of research online. If you are looking for stocks that meet certain criteria, such as my Chicken Stocks, there are many online resources that will tell you which stocks have increasing earnings, dividends, and so forth.

In addition to looking for investments, once you have picked stocks to follow, you can have updated news delivered to you. For instance, the service provided by *The Wall Street Journal* not only can deliver the paper online, but it can customize the information you receive based on your specifications. Thus, any time news breaks about your stock, you will be one of the first to know, instead of having to wait for the next

---

SOCIAL BENEFITS OF INTERNET NETWORKING

Online chat groups also serve a social function. Many new friendships revolve around a common interest, such as collecting something. Investing is an interest, too. Just as with in-person investment clubs, relationships can develop online as well. While it would be easy to say that this is a minor benefit, we are social animals. The chance to meet more people online, or even to have an activity to fill an empty life, can be very valuable to the shut-in or others without much social contact.

day's paper—in which the news may or may not be included. *The Wall Street Journal,* unlike many others that are free, is a paid service.

Rather than talking here about the massive amount of information that is available online, on pages 157–163 I list some of the many places that you can mine for information.

Lower-Cost Transactions

As mentioned at the beginning of this chapter, online investing can be less expensive than traditional means. Years ago, before commissions were deregulated, the cost for buying 100 shares of stock was generally the same no matter which stockbroker you used—and the fee could add a few percentage points to your costs. Then discount brokers emerged. They offered simple, less expensive transactions, but no research or advice. Charles Schwab is probably the largest and most successful of these discount brokers.

When transactions could be done online, it lowered the actual cost of trading. These savings were eventually passed on by some brokers in the form of still lower commissions.

> **DIRECT SALES ONLINE**
>
> Costs today are also lower for companies to issue stock (IPOs) or bonds online. If their costs of raising capital or loans are cheaper by cutting out middlemen like investment banks, they can pass along some of the savings to buyers like you, and still save money themselves. For instance, Dow Chemical was the first nonfinancial corporation to sell some of its bonds on the Internet directly to investors. They borrowed $300 million this way. A few companies have also sold stock online. But overall, this approach did not catch on in the first few years of use.

E-trade is probably the largest and most successful broker that started online.

PROBLEMS WITH ONLINE INVESTING

As mentioned at the beginning of this chapter, the two major problems with the online investing world are:

- The sheer quantity of information is so large that it is often hard to sort the "wheat from the chaff."
- There are many successful attempts at stock manipulation online.

Wrong Information Online

If you've ever been in a "chat room" about some subject you knew well, you'll know that such forums give the ignorant as well as the informed an equal chance to throw in their "two cents worth." Lots of silly questions are asked online, and lots of silly answers are given. (Put more bluntly, there are a lot of idiots spouting off.)

Don't get me wrong—there are many good things about the exchange of information online. For instance, if you have a rare disease, online is the only chance you may have to talk to hundreds of other people who have the same disease. They can give you great advice, even though everyone's experience may not apply to you. Or, if you run a dry cleaning store, the opportunity to talk to other dry cleaners online can be very valuable.

Investments are a bit different from sharing information about a common disease or business. Many times, the "chaff" from those who are wrong can overwhelm the few kernels of true wheat that can make you money. While it was easy to make money at the end of the 20th century, because stocks were going up so

> Some online firms' advertisements more closely resemble commercials for the lottery than anything else. When firms, again and again, tell investors that online investing can make them rich, it creates unrealistic expectations. In a market environment where many investors are susceptible to quixotic euphoria, I'm worried these commercials step over the line and border on irresponsibility.
>
> —Arthur Levitt, chairman of the Securities and Exchange Commission

consistently—it's still important to note that the vast majority of mutual funds didn't beat the market. If professionals working full time on the market can't outperform it, you shouldn't put much faith in anonymous postings online.

Real Costs of Transactions

Theoretically it is cheaper to buy or sell a stock online. If a full-service broker would charge $100 for a transaction, it might be possible to execute the same transaction online for $10.

> A bad execution can dwarf the commission a broker charges. You might think you are getting a good deal, but in reality, you are not.
> —Robert L.D. Colby, Securities and Exchange Commission

This looks like a big savings, and it can add up to a lot of money if you do a lot of buying and selling. There is a problem, however. Some research has shown that the price at which you buy or sell may be different using discount brokers. This is referred to technically as "execution inefficiencies."

Because deeply discounted brokers don't make much money on transactions, they can't spend much time on them. There are several ways this can cost you money. Stocks are traded differently, depending on where and when.

Cheep! Cheap isn't always cheap.

On the New York Stock Exchange, there are specialists who "make a market" buying when you sell and selling when you buy. They have been known to take advantage of knowing your order to move the price up or down, say 10 cents. This makes them a lot of money over time.

On the NASDAQ, trades are executed by computer matching run by market makers. Different market makers put in different bids to buy or sell at specific prices. If your broker doesn't take the time to look carefully, they may buy for you at a higher price than the lowest offer. Lastly, some brokers have been known to place trades through friends where they get a kickback. Again, these friends don't give you the best price.

A full-service broker can also let your order fall prey to these kinds of problems. A good one, however, knows how to avoid them. If execution problems cost you 10 cents a share, it may not be much of a problem if you only buy 100 shares. But for a larger order, the difference in execution efficiencies can easily pay for full service.

COMPUTER RESPONSE ERRORS

Surprisingly, a real problem in online trading has been *double orders*. You know how computers can be: Sometimes you double-click by accident—or sometimes on purpose, when you think your computer is not responding. That can mean two orders to buy or sell if you're online. Or, the opposite may happen—your computer may "hiccup" and not send the order you think you have entered.

If these computer errors happen to your broker, they correct them. But, if you double enter the order yourself, you are responsible for buying both orders.

ONLINE FRAUD

Unfortunately, largely because of its anonymous aspect, the Internet makes a perfect place to manipulate stocks. This is done in two general ways:
- multiple postings touting a stock
- counterfeit information released about a stock

These methods are also used together.

The Securities and Exchange Commission (SEC) is in charge of regulating the stock markets. Even with major task forces devoted to online fraud, they just don't have the time and resources to chase down the thousands of fraud cases that the Internet makes easy to carry out every month. For instance, the agency receives 200–300 complaints *per day* from investors who believe they've been cheated, yet they only handled less than 200 Internet-related enforcement cases in *three years.*

"Pump and Dump"

The major online fraud technique has also been used off-line for many years. It is usually called "pump and dump." This simply means that promoters "pump up" the interest in an obscure stock and then "dump" their shares at higher prices.

In pre-Internet days, to pump up a stock required "boiler rooms" full of people making phone calls to lists of investors. Now email, chat groups, bulletin boards, and other electronic means make it cheap and easy to claim that a new stock offering has been approved by the SEC, or that a marvelous new product will boost sales of some obscure company by a billion dollars. When you throw in links to false analysts' reports, press releases, and the like, it becomes very easy to create a picture that can look real to the investor who wants to believe that it is easy to double his or her money overnight.

TOO GOOD TO BE TRUE

Be very, very skeptical of information you receive online. People make all kinds of false claims. The most sophisticated tricksters don't come right out with bogus information, but rather, slyly drop hints about their supposed identity or the information they wish to convey. Remember, if it sounds too good to be true, chances are it is.

There are examples of these fraudulent uses of the Internet published regularly. As one newspaper reported, "Authorities say manipulating markets or illegally profiting from market swings has never been easier, faster, or cheaper."

The Examples Never Stop

How prevalent is using the Internet to run up stock prices? There aren't any statistics, but I, personally, have been approached to tout a particular stock. Here are some real examples of online fraud:

- In Raleigh, North Carolina, a 25-year-old man creates a false Web site for Bloomberg (a legitimate publisher of financial information). On it, he falsely announces that the company he works for, PairGain, has been bought. Then, in multiple chat rooms, he talks about the "deal," referring people to the bogus Web site for details and confirmation. Traders react to the "late-breaking news." PairGain shares are traded at 11 times their normal volume and the demand pushes them up 31%. He sells for a profit.

- Four students at UCLA, using campus computers and about 50 different online names, tout the shares of NEI Webworld in chat rooms. In two days, the shares go from 15 cents to $15. The students buy low and sell high, making $370,000 on the false information.

> [Recent fraud cases] are a sobering reminder for investors that on the Internet there is no clearly defined border between reliable and unreliable information. Therefore, investors must exercise extreme caution when they receive investment pitches online.
> —Richard Walker, SEC Director of Enforcement

- In Los Angeles, a former employee of an online news release service creates a fake press release for Emulex Corporation and sends it out from the service. He makes money as the stock crashes from the false news, then buys the stock at the bottom and makes more profits going up as his false news is corrected.

- Fifteen-year-old Jonathan Lebed agrees to pay back $273,000 in illegal stock market profits, plus interest. He sent hundreds of phony messages to online stock discussion groups using different names. By picking almost unknown stocks to tout, his false messages could move the market. Because of the settlement with the SEC, the teen gets to keep the profits from 16 of his 27 trades!

As the SEC steps up its attacks against online scams, those behind them find new ways to take advantage of gullible traders. For instance, *Forbes* magazine reported that scamsters like to pump stocks after regular trading hours. During this time there is less SEC oversight and less trading volume, so it is easier to move a stock's price on the lower volume. In several cases, a few promoters doubled the price of a stock after hours and then sold out. The stock went back to its regular price by the next morning.

IT'S CORNY YOLK TIME!

Cluck, cluck!

Trading online is great. I find it really speeds things up. I now lose my money five times faster than before.

* * * * *

There are three different types of investors who post on the message boards:

- Those who don't know anything: 10%
- Those who know a little: 10%
- Those who don't realize they don't know anything: 80%

—*Dimgroup.com*

Buyer Beware

These cases are examples of how people will find a way to cheat with technology.

Unfortunately, they also show how foolish people are to trade on rumors. When someone starts a rumor about a stock, you can almost count on the fact that they are doing it for their own good, not yours. Most people who tout a stock have already bought the stock and hope your later purchases will drive their stock up. Why do investors fall for these simple scams? John Coffee, Jr., a Columbia University securities law professor, says "Chat rooms are full of people just waiting to hear good news." Don't be one of them.

> *While the ability to chat online with others can be educational, eventually people want to do something, and often it gets them into trouble. Use the Internet to do research if you enjoy the process, but don't invest based on what people online tell you.*

There's almost no truly personal money advice on the Web today. In the chat rooms, you get gossip or worse. The torrent of information on stocks is just that: information— with no guidance on how the stock might fit into an investment plan.
—Jane Bryant Quinn, columnist and author

MESSAGE BOARDS AND CHAT ROOMS

Message boards allow users to post messages just like on a bulletin board. Reactions may come quickly or slowly. In chat rooms, everyone participates in "real time." I don't recommend either chat rooms or message boards as sources of information. Most of the participants are novices who know little about their topics. Other "posters" are trying to manipulate participants into buying or selling a stock so they can make a profit. (These issues were discussed earlier under "Online Problems.")

With these cautions aside, there is, of course, some educational information online. There are also cases where a stock you are interested in moves up or down in a way you can't explain. Sometimes there will be information posted which explains the move.

The four biggest sources of boards and chats as of this writing are www.quote.yahoo.com, www.fool.com, www.raging-bull.com, and www.silicon-investor.com. They can all be searched at the same time for information on a particular stock by going to www.investor.cnet.com.

ONLINE RESOURCES

The online world is fast moving. Any specific resource I mention here may have changed by the time you read this book. It is, however, easy to find sites of interest. If you enter "stock market" into most search engines, you will get listings of more sites than you have time to use. (You will also see that most of the listings are garbage, just like much of the information online.)

If you start with some of the listings on the following pages, you will find links to thousands of resources. If you're looking for additional online resources, use a "meta" search engine like www.dogpile.com that utilizes many search engines at once. You're also welcome to use the "links" section of my site (www.thesiegelgroup.com) as a starting point. I'll make sure the resources are updated as needed.

A SAMPLING OF ONLINE RESOURCES FOR INVESTORS

GENERAL INVESTMENT INFORMATION

www.thesiegelgroup.com

http://moneycentral.msn.com has lots of sample portfolios, message boards, and expert advice; links to related data, including charts, news, analyst information; a portfolio tracker; Research Wizard for evaluating companies; it can be synchronized with Microsoft Money personal-finance program.

www.quicken.com lets you exchange portfolio data between the site and Quicken personal-finance program and TurboTax; EasyStep feature walks you through the process of defining a search for a security while defining each variable; message boards; ask-the-experts boards.

www. verticalnet.com covers about 60 industries, each with a separate "community." A good way to get background for an industry you want to invest in.

www.wallstreetcity.com has lots of material, including charts. This site believes in technical analysis. Its "99-cent store" area contains analysis of stocks trading around a dollar. Different levels of paid subscriptions gives you access to a range of features.

www.forbes.com has lots of investment content.

http://aolsvc.pf.aol.com/pf/stocks/MainAmerica is America Online's Personal Finance channel (requires an AOL subscription).

www.financialengines.com works with individual investors (as well as companies and institutions). You can set your goals and receive information on financial planning, investing, and so forth.

www.bloomberg.com is a site with lots of material.

www.stockselector.com offers stock-selection tools, screens, and infor-mation on stocks with analysts' recommendations.

www.market-gauge.com shows you displays of 35 widely-used market indicators to give indications of how the market is doing.

www.marketguide.com has lots of information, varying from what happened that day to articles. It also has a tool to screen stocks based on up to 80 criteria. That is, you can ask it to list stocks that are a certain size, industry, and so forth.

www.abovetrade.com covers charting. This site doesn't deal with the fundamentals of stocks and value. It looks for, and allows you to look for, stocks that have had certain types of chart action. For instance, it will give you a stock's price and its moving average over a past period. Technical systems believe a stock should be above its moving average (showing momentum) to be a "buy."

www.clearstation.com shows you the picks and performance of ama-teur stock pickers. There are also links for information about the stocks, and discussion groups about the market.

www.valuestocks.net is an example of a site by an amateur investor. This MD shows his portfolio and analysis approach. Lots of links to books for more information.

www.investhelp.com has information on stock splits and other material.

www.finance.yahoo.com and www.quote.yahoo.com give stock prices back to 1984; also investment news, research, SEC filings, financials, historical quotes, charts, editorial analysis, chat rooms, and discussion forums.

www.investing.lycos.com includes quotes, basic charts, and Quote.com's Live Charts (free for delayed data).

www.stockpoint.com provides a good blend of news, data, and tools.

www.whitehouse.gov includes the latest economic statistics issued by the government. To find them, enter "Economic Statistics" in the search feature at the left of the page.

www.fool.com includes market and data, both real-time and historical; investing fundamentals, quotes and charts, and model portfolios.

www.multexinvestor.com is a *Forbes* magazine favorite for finding brokerage research on companies. Summary estimates and brief company descriptions are free; detailed reports are pay-per-view. Free trials are available from some brokers.

www.clearstation.com has a three-pronged approach to investing that balances fundamental, technical, and community information to evaluate potential investments. "Tag & Bag" screens securities for technical or fundamental events; you can "subscribe" to other members' portfolios, and watch what members and the Clearstation experts are recommending.

www.iexchange.com lets you post your stock picks. The site then tracks your performance. If your track record is good, you can start selling reports to visitors to the site.

www.investools.com gives you dozens of industry newsletters as a registered free user. There is a monthly charge for additional features, many that you can find free elsewhere.

www.briefing.com provides quotes, charts, and an economic calendar for free. Paid subscriptions for additional information and tools (some of which you can get for free elsewhere).

www.thomsoninvest.net is a good place to find breaking news. I-Watch is a graphical representation of interest and buy/sell messages sent by institutional traders during a purchase decision.

www.thestreet.com has breaking news and analysis. Breaks out news on tech-stocks, mutual funds, and international investments separate from other market coverage. Market primers cover investing basics, research tools, portfolio tracker, , financials and profiles, plus charts.

www.investorama.com has links to more than 14,000 financial sites and lots of information.

www.morningstar.com has a great Portfolio Manager and Annualizer. Pay features (currently $9.95 a month or $99 a year) include advanced asset-allocation tools, stock screening, and real-time analysis and news.

www.siliconinvestor.com has news, charts, discussion boards, company profiles, SEC filings, and past and present financials. Multex provides some free broker research; there is a fee charged for other research. Also has free email and personal calendar features.

FOR SPECIFIC RESEARCH

www.bigcharts.com specializes in customizable charting. It also lists the 10 best and 10 worst performing industries for time spans varying from one week up to five years. My favorite for a quick look at a company.

www.hoovers.com provides details on companies. In their Company Capsule summaries, it also lists the top three competitors of a company. Its reports that cover more than 50,000 public and private companies in more than 300 industries. One of the best, but much of the information must be purchased ($14.95 a month for unlimited access).

www.fundalarm.com is a free, noncommercial Website that provides a formula for helping people decide when to consider selling a mutual fund. Provides a "three-alarm system" to pinpoint a fund that has underperformed its benchmark for the past 12 months, three years, and five years.

www.ipo.com lists initial public offerings.

www.bestcalls.com provides lists of calls coming up. You can search by company name, receive emails when a call of interest in pending.

www.lanston.com is the site of Aubrey G. Lanston, the venerable dealer in US government securities.

www.yardeni.com is from Ed Yardeni, chief economist of Deutsche Banc Alex Brown. You can request an annotated version of key economic releases via fax.

www.iqc.com (IqChart) has technical-analysis charts that update in real time, for $24.95 a month.

TO BUY/SELL STOCKS

E-trade (www.etrade.com) Probably the biggest online broker. Lots of information.

Sharebuilder.com helps you invest directly in stocks at a low cost. About 1500 or so companies sell stock direct to shareholders or the public at no, or very low, cost. These DRIP plans (Direct Investment Plans) are great for investors who want to put a few dollars a month into stocks. For instance, they work well for children. Sharebuilder.com does the same thing for companies that don't offer their shares directly. For $2 per transaction, you can invest any amount of money in specific stocks.

NEWS

www.cbsmarketwatch.com has a portfolio tracker, links for fundamental data, earnings, charts, news stories, discussion forums, streaming real-time quotes, and a thorough investing primer. They have great articles but most of their news is seen towards the end of the day.

www.ft.com (Financial Times) is the best source for international news, data, and commentary; specializes in global investment news.

www.worldlyinvestor.com has investing news and commentary on the Americas, Asia, Europe, and emerging markets; also quotes and rankings; and a few tools like message boards and a portfolio tracker.

www.adr.com lets you search its database by company to get fundamental data, estimates, news, charts, and other financials. Also provides overviews by region and industry.

www.global-investor.com has news, links, and other resources relevant to international investing.

www.theflyonthewall.com has staffers that spend their days collecting tidbits from sources like companies themselves, brokers, trading desks, money managers, and other intermediaries. The information isn't always accurate; sometimes it's confirmed factual information, and sometimes rumors. The tab is steep: $49.99 a month, or $479.90 a year.

TAX INFORMATION

www.fairmark.com has information on tax issues related to stock purchases and sales.

GENERAL FINANCIAL PLANNING INFORMATION

www.ihatefinancialplanning.com

www.adviceamerica.com

www.efmoody.com

www.directadvice.com

BASIC INFORMATION FOR YOUNG INVESTORS

Some basic financial information that may be useful for your children or grandchildren is included in these sites.

www.acecusa.org

www.fl2001.org

www.investor.nasd.com/teach

www.nice.emivh.edu

www.edgate.com

www.financiallearning.com

http://smithbarney.com/yin

www.fleetkids.com

www.mainxchange.com

www.thinkquest.com

www.younginvestor.com

COVERAGE OF NEWER INDUSTRIES

www.technewsworld.com has lots of high-tech news stories.

www.bullmarket.com provides free weekly online newsletters on the biotech and wireless communication industries, among others.

www.biospace.com is the place for biotechnology news.

www.drugtopics.com has news about the pharmaceutical industry.

FOREIGN INVESTMENT INFORMATION

www.worldlyinvestor.com is a major source of international investment information.

www.europeaninvestor.com covers exchange rates and European investments.

www.nni.nikkei.co.jp is from a Japanese newspaper and covers Asian business news.

www.patagon.com covers South American financial information.

SUMMARY

I've pointed out in this chapter that, on the one hand, online investing has many attractive benefits while, on the other hand, it is fraught with perils. If you make your own investment decisions and want to handle your own trades, online investing can save you money. It is very risky, however, to believe what you read online. Despite the large amount of useful research information available online, there is even more garbage, hype, ignorance, and outright lies.

If you wish to use online resources, I've given you some good starting points. The Internet moves fast, but even if some of the sites I list have changed, you will find thousands by following the links from one site to another and doing some basic searches. Be careful and good hunting.

11

WHEN THE MARKET CRASHES
Fads, "Bubbles," High Tech IPOs, and the Like

The very word "panic" denotes a fear so great as to make those who experience it to become for the time being crazy...
—THEODORE ROOSEVELT

THE WORST FEAR OF EVERY investor is a market crash—and the worst thing about crashes is that they seem to happen when everyone is the most optimistic. Actually, one of the big factors that signals a crash is when "everyone" thinks the market will go up "forever."

A 20% decline is considered a bear market. Surprisingly, there is no clearly accepted definition of the term "crash" to distinguish it from a bear market. I would like to offer one to help clarify the term. A crash is a 20% or greater decline in stock prices over a short period of time. For major market indexes such as NASDAQ, the Dow Jones Industrial Average, or the Standard & Poor's 500, the decline must occur over a two-week period or less. The purest example of a crash occurs on a single day.

WHEN STOCKS ARE OVERVALUED

The stock market often gives signals that it is vulnerable for a crash. If you remember my discussion of price earning ratios in Chapter 2, you might recall that PE ratios are a way of valuing stocks. When stocks are booming, the most popular companies often sell at 100 or more times earnings—or even have no earnings (such was the case with many Internet companies in 2000). These PE multiples can only be sustained if the stocks' earnings (or sales) grow very fast. Since this seldom happens in the long run, stock prices always come down after reaching these extremes. The classic overvaluation was, of course, 1929.

What, exactly, did happen in 1929?

MARKET PSYCHOSIS

When talking about the stock market, just the mention of the year 1929 reminds people of the horrible stock market plummet that defines the term crash. As mentioned in Chapter 1, most people's fears about the market trace back to the crash of 1929. I like to call that the "Great American Financial Psychosis."

Let's briefly relive history to outline what

1929 STOCK MARKET CRASH

"Black Thursday"

350

300

250

200

JUL AUG SEP OCT NOV DEC

happened in 1929—as well as some things that did not happen that everyone believes are true. The crash was *not* caused by the Depression; it actually came before the Depression. While the story is complicated, the crash was caused by international trade tariffs and interest rate meddling by governments. Money was backed by gold in those days. This tended to keep governments from printing paper money with no value (a practice that causes inflation).

GOVERNMENT MEDDLING

In some ways, the 1929 Crash started with Great Britain. In 1927, Britain lowered their interest rates in order to stimulate their economy. (Making money cheaper encourages borrowing and spending.) Because lowering interest rates is inflationary, investors moved gold out of England to France and America and converted the pound into francs and dollars.

To stop this outflow, the Bank of England persuaded the US Federal Reserve Bank to lower our interest rates, making our dollars less attractive to British gold. (You'll notice in the news today that governments are still trying to convince each other to raise or lower interest rates to achieve some theoretical "ideal balance" between countries in currency values and trade. It still doesn't work very well in the long run!)

Cheaper money was inflationary and encouraged people to spend money. The

WHAT IS A PONZI SCHEME?

Charles Ponzi collected money from investors with promises of big returns. Then he used money from later investors to pay large dividends to early investors. This created more demand to invest from these early investors and their friends, which, in turn, was used to pay more dividends. As long as enough new investors were coming in, Ponzi could pay off older investors with part of the new money and live high on the rest. This is also called a "pyramid scheme" because it takes a lot of later investors to support the earlier ones.

Dow Jones stock average went from well under 200 in 1927 to a peak of almost 400 in September 1929 before the crash. (The actual gains were 149% in two years.) When the market starts to go up so dramatically, it attracts new investors who follow the trends. Like a Ponzi Scheme, where early profits attract later suckers, rising markets attract more money and enthusiasm, which in turn makes more people want to jump on board before they miss out. Some "high tech" stocks of the '20s—like radio—gained 500% or more.

MARGIN BUYING

Much of this frantic buying of stocks was made possible by easily borrowed money. "Margin buying" today means that you can buy $2 worth of stock for $1 by borrowing the other dollar from your broker. This is called a 50% margin rate because you have to put up 50% of the money. This gives you twice the profit on your money. If a stock goes up 50%, you gain 100% on your money minus a small interest payment. The table shows how this works.

	Buying on Margin	Straight Investment
Cost of 100 shares at $10/share:	$1000	$1000
You invest:	$500	$1000
You borrow from broker:	$500	
You sell stock at $15/share	$1500	$1500
Interest on $500 loan from broker	$20	$0
Profit	$480	$500
% profit on investment (profit ÷ money *you* invested)	96%	50%

Today's margin rates of 50% were created because of the role margin rates played in the Crash of 1929. In 1928, you could borrow 95% of the money used for the purchase of stocks! That means that every dollar you put up could buy $20 worth of stock! By 1929, margin rates were raised to 20% in an effort to slow down the speculation. Even at that rate, however, it meant that every dollar could buy $5 worth of stock. This is still a lot of speculative buying power.

MOMENTUM "BAND WAGON" BUYING

From 1927 to 1929, everyone wanted to get in on the incredible growth in stocks. Since the market is determined by supply and demand, stock prices were pushed up. And, since so many people wanted to buy stock, more was created for them to buy.

"And now from our self-fulfilling prophesy newsroom, here's the latest on the recession."

Some of the worst offenders were called closed-end investment companies back then (similar to mutual funds today). These companies would sell stock to raise money to buy the stocks of other companies. This brought even more money into the market and created more buying pressure. In the worst cases, funds were buying other funds, who in turn bought other funds, and so on.

The more stocks went up, the easier it seemed to be to make money, and the more people jumped in. And, of course, many *did* make a lot of money in the market. When stocks double, many great stories develop of tremendous profits. Most of the late-comers knew nothing about the market or the companies they bought. They just followed tips and rumors. Back in those days, there was less regulation of the market, so more people could "hype" the value of stocks that were worthless.

The ignorant and unrestrained enthusiasm was a key indicator that the market was dangerously high. There is a cute story that when one Wall Street bigwig (Joseph Kennedy, President John F. Kennedy's father) heard his shoe-shine boy giving stock tips, the Wall Streeter immediately sold his stocks, thus saving his millions a couple of months before the crash.

PANIC SELLING

Just as momentum and enthusiasm build on the up side to overvalue stocks, the same thing happens on the down side. Once stocks fell 10% or more, it tended to scare some people out of the market and keep others from coming in. This tended to depress demand for stocks. When stocks start to fall, brokers issue "margin calls" to investors who have bought stocks on margin. These investors then have to come up with more money because their holdings are worth less. The typical rule today is that an investor is required to maintain positive value in their account of 30% or more, even when a stock goes down. (See the table on the opposite page.)

> The investment business is, by definition, a business of hope. Everyone hopes that he can beat the market, even if few people actually can.
> —Avi Nachmany, *The Only Guide to Winning Investment Strategy*

BUYING ON MARGIN

Cost of 100 shares at $10/share	$1000
You invest:	$500
You borrow from broker:	$500
Stock falls to $5 share; value of stock is:	$500
Stock is now worth $500; you owe the the broker $500; therefore, the value of your account is:	$0
Broker issues margin call for new $300 deposit from you to maintain a positive value	

With the 5%–20% margin rates of the 1920s, investors would have been asked for even *more* money much sooner. And in some cases, brokers sold the stock to cover margins without checking with customers. (That's their right under the margin agreements. This still happens, such as during the 2000 "wreck of high tech.") When a margin call comes, some people don't want to put more money into the market, or don't have it. So they sell their stocks. This causes stock prices to drop more. Thus, the downward spiral continues—the reverse of what happened on the upside.

IT CAN'T HAPPEN HERE

In the 1920s, as happens before most crashes, many "experts" stated that stocks were likely to go permanently up because "we are in a new era." For instance, just before the crash, a Yale professor said "Stock prices have reached what looks like a permanent high plateau." Of course, Professor Fisher was also promoting an investment company that raised investment money to put in the stock market! You have to beware of who's promoting a stock or the market. It's well known that most analysts who issue expert opinions on stocks today seldom rate stocks a "sell" (as mentioned in Chapter 9 on Hired Help).

A DIFFERENT PERSPECTIVE

At this point, most history simply states that, from the peak in October 1929 to the bottom in 1932, the Dow Jones was down 89%, so people lost 89% of their money. While the facts are true, the market did not go down consistently after the first crash. In fact, there were multiple rallies. Many people tried valiantly to support the prices of key stocks to stem the tide of panic (and generally lost money for their efforts).

There were very few people jumping out of windows. That is one of the cultural myths that was used to "brand" this event and create the investment phobia discussed in Chapter 1. Many people didn't lose much money in 1929. They lost their money over the next two years buying "bargains" and trying to anticipate the next big rally.

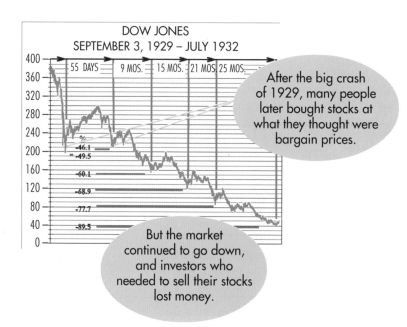

DOW JONES
SEPTEMBER 3, 1929 – JULY 1932

After the big crash of 1929, many people later bought stocks at what they thought were bargain prices.

But the market continued to go down, and investors who needed to sell their stocks lost money.

WHEN IS THE MARKET TOO HIGH?

It's easy to say after the fact that the market was too high and then crashed. But, when you're in the middle of it and it takes two and a half years to fully play out, the picture is not so clear. When you look at a detailed chart of the price changes after the crash, you see that the market was up and down several times.

> A boom is a situation in which over-optimism triumphs over a rate of interest which, in a cooler light, would be seen to be excessive.
>
> —John Maynard Keynes

WILL THIS MARKET GO UP OR DOWN?

Technical analysts claim to be able to tell when the market is poised for a downturn. But, while the downturn is happening, it is impossible to tell whether it is the start of a pull back, or a "pause that refreshes" before a rally resumes. A plateau can last for years. There was much the same problem interpreting market direction in 2000 and 2001 as shown below.

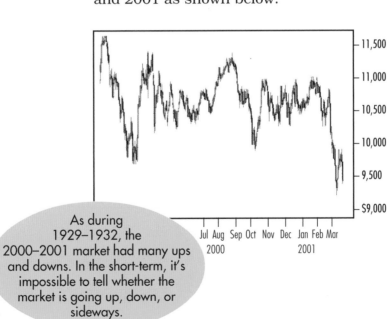

As during 1929–1932, the 2000–2001 market had many ups and downs. In the short-term, it's impossible to tell whether the market is going up, down, or sideways.

The good news about the 1929 crash is that it stimulated a number of reforms that make it harder for the same types of problems to occur again at that level. For instance, as already mentioned, many regulations were changed, such as margin requirements being raised to 50%.

IT <u>WILL</u> HAPPEN AGAIN

While some reforms help tone down crashes like the one in 1929, it has happened over and over both before *and* after that well known date.

Before the crash of 1929, there had been panics and crashes in our stock market that were almost as big about every 20 years (1819, 1837, 1857, 1873, 1883, 1893, 1907). It may be that when a stock market crash happens, the shock makes people remember for a generation, or it may take a few years for an economic recovery to lay the foundation for the next boom and overvaluation.

After the crash of 1929, there were many other crashes (such as those in 1973 and 1987) in the market. The most recent at this writing was the year 2000 in high tech stocks. While the general indexes went down about 20% at that time, high tech and other speculative indexes went down about 60% overall.

We can be sure that there will be more ups and downs. The crashes will come when

CORRECT PREDICTIONS ARE OFTEN RANDOM

"Even a stopped clock is right twice a day." This old saying is well to keep in mind when the latest "expert" makes an accurate prediction. They don't publicize the 20 times they were wrong and the media doesn't publicize the other 1000 people who were wrong. By chance, somebody will always be right at any point in time.

stocks are valued at all-time highs and many experts offer justifications for prices being extra high "because things are different *this* time!"

There will also be many years when stocks are higher than they should be by traditional valuations and they don't crash immediately. Before the big Japanese crash, stocks and real estate were overvalued for years. And before the high tech crash of 2000, computer-related stocks had been flying high for about two years. If you're a smart "cowardly investor," you'll hold stocks for the long run and not get carried away by the overvaluations of stocks *or* by the crashes.

Some people believe that there are magical "cycles" or "waves" of economic ups and downs. After the fact, some pattern always emerges. The fact that, for many years, the market went up after a National Football Conference team won the Superbowl, is pure coincidence (and the pattern finally broke). After the fact, it is always possible to relate a crash or boom to *something*.

> ### THERE ARE ALSO CRASHES IN FOREIGN MARKETS
>
> The Nikkei 225 represents the Japanese stock market in the same way the Dow Jones Industrial Average represents US stocks. At the end of December, 1989, the Nikkei 225 peaked at 38,915. By August 1992, the Nikkei had dropped 63% to 14,194. This classic crash in the Japanese market has had effects well past the year 2000.

OTHER FAMOUS "BUBBLES"

Big overvaluations of stocks and other assets are often referred to as "bubbles" because they must pop after they grow too big. Some of the early bubbles make interesting historical reading. We can learn from them because the psychological factors behind them are still with us today. Sir Isaac Newton said, "I can calculate the motions of heavenly bodies, but not the madness of people," in referring to such speculative behavior. His quote would have been a lot wiser, except for the fact that shortly after he said it he lost big money in the speculation around the South Sea Bubble!

The classic reference on bubbles and crashes is Charles Mackay's 1841 book *Extraordinary Popular Delusions and the Madness of Crowds*. In fact, I'm happy to say that my wife gave me a first edition for our anniversary. In it, Mackay describes the Dutch tulip bulb mania, the Mississippi Bubble, and the South Sea Bubble as the main examples of the "madness of crowds" in the financial area.

Tulip Bulbs

Tulips were brought to Europe from Turkey in about 1550. By 1634, they had become status symbols of the wealthy, particularly in Holland. So, naturally, the middle classes and merchants wanted to get in on owning rare tulip bulbs. For about two years, a "stock market" was run for tulip bulbs and it soared.

By 1636 when the tulip market crashed, tulips were being traded on the Amsterdam Stock Exchange and other exchanges! In fact, a futures market was also invented, with people promising to deliver a certain type of tulip bulb at a specific price in the future.

As reports of instant wealth became common,

> ### BUY TULIPS, GET RICH
>
>
>
> "At first, as in all these gambling mania, confidence was at its height and everybody gained. The tulip-jobbers speculated in the rise and fall of the tulip stocks, and made large profits by buying when prices fell, and selling out when they rose. Many individuals grew suddenly rich. A golden bait hung temptingly out before the people, and one after the other, they rushed to the tulip-marts, like flies around a honey-pot."
> —Charles Mackay,
> *Extraordinary Popular Delusions and the Madness of Crowds*

people sold property or mortgaged their houses to buy rare tulip bulbs. At the peak, a particular bulb sold for the equivalent of about $25,000. And after the crash, that same bulb fell about 90%. This is recorded as the first major crash of modern history.

As with most speculations, the banks made loans to people who wanted to buy tulips. Easier credit caused general inflation and the cost of living soared. After the crash there was also general deflation. The courts refused to enforce tulip futures contracts, calling them gambling debts—so many people were ruined.

> One of my clients, just before transferring to me, bought a "hot" IPO, Valinix Systems, at $280 a share. Twelve months later, it was selling for $2.85 a share.
>
> — Fred Siegel

We'd Never Fall for That Today!

The nice thing about the tulip mania is that it is now easy to sit back and say, "I'd never pay so much for one flower." How could an entire country and financial system come to ruin because of tulips! The same argument, however, can be made for overpaying for shares of a company that has no income, just a hope of developing an online business. In 2000, many initial public offerings (IPOs) of dot-com businesses went from $15 to $100 on the first day of trading. A few months later, they crashed, falling 50–90%. And now some are out of business.

Values Are Arbitrary

It's always easy to wonder how a collector could pay thousands of dollars for something that we don't care about—like tulips, or stamps, or Beanie Babies. But what makes a picture of water lilies by Monet worth $10 million, or even $45 million?

Value in collectibles depends on what people are willing to pay. Values are always arbitrary. If you expect the asset to go up, it is a reason to pay more for it. In business valuation, this is called the current value of future expected earnings. Fortunately, with good stocks, you have real earnings to value and good reason to expect future earnings to continue to go up.

One good result did come from the Tulip Mania, in addition to a financial lesson that has endured for hundreds of years. Holland continued to cultivate tulips and to develop markets for the flowers. Like windmills, tulips are a charming part of Holland's landscape today, as well as a grim reminder of the less charming part of human nature.

The Mississippi Bubble

The Mississippi Bubble was a scam rather than just speculative stupidity. John Law, a compulsive gambler, fled to France after killing a man in a duel over a lover. In 1716, he was granted a license to set up a bank. At the time, France was in a depression of sorts and had just devalued its currency by reducing the precious metals content. In contrast, Law's bank issued paper money backed completely by gold and silver. In addition, he proclaimed that a banker should be shot if he issued currency without 100% backing by precious metals.

Soon, the official French currency had fallen 80% in

JOHN LAW

value and Law's money traded at a premium to it. Then, the politicians convinced him to become a government institution and he started issuing money with no backing at all. With more money in circulation, interest rates fell and an inflationary boom ensued.

As part of his deal with the government, Law created a "Mississippi Company" and sold stock in the company. France granted it the exclusive rights to trade on the Mississippi River. Remember, the French owned the Louisiana Territory at this time, and had commerce from Canada to New Orleans. Rather than focusing on actual trade, they circulated continual rumors that there was gold to be had for the taking in America.

THE GREATER FOOL THEORY

When prices are soaring, at first the problem is one of supply. If you have a stock, or a house on the water in California, or a tulip bulb that many people want, people with more dollars than sense bid against each other to get it. And it can make sense to pay a lot for a popular "beanie baby" or tulip, *as long as other people are still crazy to get them*, because there will always be a greater fool to buy at a higher price. The problem, of course, is that eventually people come to their senses, the fad passes, and the last holders are stuck with no one to sell to while prices are crashing.

If It Sounds Too Good to Be True... Then the real scam began. To make the stock more attractive, Law promised a yearly dividend of 40%. This was as outrageously high then as it would be today.

As if this weren't enough, Law told investors he would help reduce the French national debt so they could buy their stock with the French currency, not precious metals. But the dividend was to be paid in gold or silver, so subscribers would end up converting deflated currency into gold and silver worth much more! This ended up valuing the annual dividend (the 40% dividend plus the currency gain) at 120% of the investment cost. Naturally, people plunged in since it would only take one year to more than pay for their investment and the rest would be pure gravy!

Each issue of stock sold out. And later issues sold out even though the price was raised 1000%. (Sounds a bit like IPO fever, doesn't it!). Speculation went wild, and general inflation drove prices in much of France up 100% a month for months. The feeling of instant wealth was everywhere and a spending boom looked like real prosperity with new houses, clothing sales, and luxury goods booming.

The boom ended in 1720 when the first person demanded massive redemption of his notes for gold and silver. A run on the bank ensued and Law's businesses collapsed. The collapse in the stock price was 99% and the French economy sank once more into a depression.

The South Sea Bubble

In 1711, the Earl of Oxford floated the new South Sea Company in Great Britain. He invited holders of nine million pounds worth of British government bonds to exchange them for stock in the new company. In return for retiring this part of the national debt—when the pound was really worth something—he was granted a monopoly on British trade with South America and the "South Sea Islands." The fact that the Spanish and Portuguese had that area pretty well sewn up was overlooked!

> The circumstances that induce the recurrent lapses into financial dementia have not changed in any truly operative fashion since the Tulip-mania of 1636-1637.
> — John Kenneth Galbraith

Nothing happened with the stock until 1720 when the Earl offered to trade South Sea's stock for 31 million pounds of British bonds—essentially the whole national debt at the time. Wiser heads argued against the deal as a stock manipulation. But, rumors started by the Earl claimed that England was negotiating with Spain for free trade, that gold and silver from South America would flood England, and that the stock would pay yearly dividends equivalent to the basic price of the stock.

South Sea stock soared from 128 pounds to 1000 pounds in six months! Even opponents who had pointed out that the promised returns were impossible climbed on board. And this may be the big lesson from bubbles. When everyone around you is "getting in on the next great thing," you don't want to be left out, whether it's worthless swampland in Florida or the latest new stock issue that will change the world with high technology.

Naturally, the South Sea Bubble collapsed. The Bank of England refused to redeem their bank notes in precious metals as promised, and a five-year boom crashed into depression.

IT'S HAPPENED BEFORE

"...mania is the only way to describe it...companies are merging in a desperate search for efficiency, market share, new products and technology. Fueling it all is a strong stock market." Sounds current, doesn't it? It sounds like it was written in the early part of 2000, but it's actually from *The Wall Street Journal*—in 1901!

Blind Pools

The general euphoria in England created dozens of other new companies organized for speculative purposes. The most outrageous promised that, for every two pounds invested, subscribers would receive 100 pounds a year in dividends from a company that was so secret they couldn't tell investors what they were going to do! In one day, the promoter collected 2000 pounds and skipped to Europe!

While you may think you'd never fall for such silliness, think again. There is still a class of companies called blind pools where the money is raised to purchase working companies, but they are not allowed by law to say what companies they will purchase. One professor in the Stanford MBA program helped many students set up these pools. While some of them worked out, giving your money to a new MBA to spend on an unknown company "because they could manage it better" certainly has considerable danger.

IT CAN HAPPEN HERE!

After reading about several of these crashes, you've probably noticed that it's the same cycle repeated again and again. Speculators pump up some ridiculous idea enough that early players realize profits. Once the momentum begins, fueled by rumors, more money chases the opportunity.

Eventually, people start to realize that it can't keep going up because there is no underlying value. Once people start to pull

UPS AND DOWNS ARE "NATURAL"

Renowned economist Joseph Schumpeter, and many others who study economic cycles, believes that recurrent mania is a normal feature of business life. Economists' records of prediction of value during bubbles are terrible. And while they always have an explanation *after the fact*, often different schools of thought can't even agree about what happened! Perhaps much of the problem is that they fail to accurately factor in investor *psychology*, which is much more complicated than the flow of dollars and industry!

out, there is a monster crash. People are ruined, banks and governments renege on their promises, and it takes years to recover. Or as famous economist John Kenneth Galbraith said, "All financial innovation involves, in one form or another, the creation of debt secured in greater or lesser adequacy by real assets... All crises have involved debt that, in one fashion or another, has become dangerously out of scale in relation to the underlying means of payment."

You'd never get carried away like that, would you?

The earliest and most famous bubbles were European mistakes. But, we in the US have had plenty of our own. Galbraith also concludes that there is nothing that can be done to stop such craziness: "Recurrent descent into insanity is not a wholly attractive feature of capitalism. [Enhanced skepticism is warranted] when a mood of excitement pervades a market or surrounds an investment prospect, when there is a claim of unique opportunity based on a special foresight, all sensible people should circle the wagons; it is time for caution."

IT'S CORNY YOLK TIME

Cluck, cluck!

One theory of the stock market ties the rise and fall of stock prices to the rise and fall of women's hemlines. Proof of this phenomenon is in the following historical facts: Glamour stocks and mini skirts soared in 1993. Conglomerates and hemlines went down in the spring of 1994. Hot pants led the Dow Jones up in 1971.

The advice to the investor then, is, "Don't sell until you see the heights of their thighs!"

The Canal Boom

Today we've forgotten such prosaic means of travel as canals, except in the song about the Erie Canal. But in the 1830s, canals played an important role in opening the "West" (at that time referring to the western parts of the eastern states and anything further west.) Investment in land around the US looked good enough for British banks to finance a speculative flurry of canal and turnpike building.

In 1837, the crash came and the governments of Pennsylvania, Mississippi, Indiana, Maryland, Louisiana, and Michigan all repudiated their debts for canals as other infrastructures. In fact, Galbraith reports that the states expressed anger that the foreign banks and investors would expect repayment after the crash for debts so foolishly granted! He further suggests that much of today's Third World debt may be similar (both in foolish grants and unlikelihood of repayment).

> The more things change, the more they stay the same.
> —Parmenides

The Florida Land Boom

One of the signs of dangerous speculation before the crash of 1929 was the promotion of Florida land. You still occasionally hear people today refer to buying "Florida swampland" just as they refer to buying the Brooklyn Bridge—as examples of crooked salesmen or stupid buyers.

The climate in Florida was an improvement over the frigid Eastern seaboard. And today, of course, Florida is well developed— one might say overdeveloped. But, in the 1920s, it wasn't much. Like any bubble, promoters started building up the value of lots in Florida. They were generally said to be near the ocean or a major city. This often meant they were in a swamp miles from the ocean, or 50 miles from a small city at a time when roads were poorly developed.

By creating a market for Florida land, and promoting it, the shysters were able to produce quick profits for early buyers. Soon, buyers were buying only for the purposes of selling to the next person coming along (the Greater Fool Theory). Even the famous Charles Ponzi was able to sell Florida land—and this was *after* he'd been convicted for inventing the Ponzi Scheme named in his "honor."

As with every bubble, prices soared ridiculously and wiser heads began to see that there was no economic reason behind the run-up. In 1925, two major hurricanes hit Florida and destroyed today's equivalent of billions in property value. This ended the boom in Florida land. While nature took the blame in this case, the bust was already inevitable when the hurricanes hit.

> Those who cannot remember the past are condemned to repeat it.
> —George Santayana

WHAT ABOUT TOMORROW?

So, what do we learn from this long—and hopefully interesting—discussion of the history of market bubbles and crashes?

We know large overvaluations and subsequent market crashes have happened regularly and will happen again. We have only to look at the huge rise and 60+% losses in Internet and many other computer-related stocks in 1999–2001 to see that nothing has changed.

Two things can save you from being carried away by the next "tulip mania:"

- remembering the lessons of history that even good investments can be too expensive when their cost is far too high to allow them to provide a reasonable return, and
- having an investment philosophy that will insulate you from passing fads.

A SOUND INVESTMENT PHILOSOPHY

In the long term, the stock market will give you a superior return to other investments of equal quality and liquidity. By selecting from among my Chicken Stocks, and by following other approaches recommended in this book, you can have this superior return with great confidence.

FOREVER BUBBLES				
YEAR(S)	MANIA	LOCATION	RUN-UP	DECLINE
1634–37	Tulip bulbs	Holland	5,900%	93%
1719–20	South Sea shares	Britain	1,000%	84%
1921–29	American stocks	US	497%	87%
1965–89	Japanese stocks	Japan	3,270%	63%
1979–82	Silver	US	710%	88%
1990-2000	NASDAQ	US	1460%	68%

Source: PrudentBear.com

In the shorter term, however, we will have crashes. Depending on how you measure, the stock market had one long and dramatic increase for the last 25 years of the 20th century. It is possible that, like the Japanese market after its crash from ridiculous heights in 1990, the NASDAQ or other parts of the American market could have several years of sidewise movement in the early years of the 21st century. The crash of many high tech stocks in early 2000 could have an effect on other sectors for many years.

It takes nerves of steel, or a mature, long-term perspective, to deal with crashes and hypes. But, if you take the long view, and don't get distracted by fads of the moment, you will make money over time.

As discussed in the next chapter, my Chicken Stock approach is a special form of growth investing. If you agree with my philosophy to buy pieces of great companies with outstanding long-term records of earnings *and* dividend increases, I don't think you can go wrong. But there will be many voices trying to get you to buy the next "tulip bulb." Develop your own philosophy of investing and it will help you see the long-term value of owning part of America. If you find yourself wavering and drawn to the newest fad, read this book again. While I'm biased, I agree with some of the book's early reviewers who said it would be a good idea to give a copy to one's children or grandchildren to help them have a sounder grasp of the investment world.

SUMMARY

The dramatic stock market crash in 1929 seared itself on the minds of investors for generations. It is responsible for the financial phobia many people continue to have about the stock market. Taking a closer look, however, shows us that the 1929 crash did not come as a big surprise to knowledgeable investors. There were plenty of signs before the crash for conservative investors.

And there was plenty of time *after* "the crash" for investors to get out of the market with most of their money.

While the 1929 Crash, and subsequent Depression, was a big event in our financial history, it was just one example of many. There are many factors that make a crash the size of the Great Depression unlikely, but there will be more "boom and bust" cycles. By staying with sound, long-term strategies such as I describe in this book, and staying away from fads, your investments can repay you and your family well.

12

WHERE DO YOU GO FROM HERE?

Money is like an arm or a leg—use it or lose it.
—HENRY FORD

THIS BOOK WAS DESIGNED TO be easy to read. In some ways it is elementary, but I have also covered some fairly sophisticated concepts in what I hope is an easy-to-understand manner. If you've read this far, you know more—or have access to more information—than 95% of investors.

WHAT'S NEXT?

Ken Blanchard, the "One Minute Manager," says that, in the business world, too many people study a subject and then say, "Okay, what's next?" rather than applying what they have learned. The same is true of investing. If you want to see superior long-term results for your investments, you should apply what you've learned from this book rather than moving on to the next investing fad.

SEEK PROFITS, NOT EXCITEMENT

The biggest mistake most active investors make is taking action because they are bored. Rather than be content with a good approach, they look for excitement by trying something new. This is a disaster for long-term investing success. If you find something that makes sense for you and works, stick with it.

Most of my clients don't want to be preoccupied with the market and different investment strategies. They want to reap the long-term rewards of beating the market, and to be able to sleep at night without worry.

As discussed in Chapter 1, you need to develop your own investment philosophy and then implement it. In this book, I've recommended my Chicken Stock approach for long-term growth investing. I've covered other strategies as well. The right kind of annuities can be a good strategy for super

WHY INVESTORS FAIL

"Investing is 90% emotional. I now believe that the biggest reason investors fail isn't a lack of knowledge, but an excess of emotion. We often don't have enough self-discipline when it comes to spending and saving. We are far too confident in our ability to pick winning investments and forecast markets. We fret too much over short-term performance, even though we are supposedly investing for the next 30 years. Successful investing…is about devising a plan that allows you to meet your long-term financial goals, without panicking during short-term market turbulence."

—Jonathan Clements,
The Wall Street Journal

cowards. If you need extra income now, bonds might be the approach to take.

Some of the other investment opportunities I've covered—such as traditional mutual funds—I don't recommend for most people. As discussed in Chapters 4 and 5, unit trusts are often the better choice.

WHAT DO YOU NEED?

Now might be a good time to review your answers to the questions in Chapter 1. I asked how you felt about risk and the stock market, what were your needs for income now and later, and so forth.

> If you haven't already, now would be a good time to fill out the worksheets on pages 15–17.

Now that you've read this book, I hope you are less fearful of investing. The more you know about something, the more comfortable you usually are with it. You wouldn't have read this book if you didn't want to increase your understanding of, and comfort with, investment principles.

After some analysis of your situation—such as how much income you need now and later—your key decision is whether to move forward and implement a consistent program for yourself and your estate. By "program," I mean a program you can stay with for years, if not decades.

INVESTMENT RISK AND YOUR RETURN

In analyzing your investment situation and your own psychology, you need to think about the risk/reward trade-off. A key concept about investment risk is that you "pay" for safety. The safer the investment, the less total return you normally earn. It won't always work out this way, because the return is based on the expected risk and return—which may or may not be what actually happens in the future. Starting with the least risk, here is a review of the types of investments that you could use:

1 GUARANTEED VARIABLE ANNUITIES FROM STRONG INSURANCE COMPANIES. As of the writing of this book, choosing a good product could give you the best of either a guaranteed 6% annual return or the stock market's performance, whichever is better, with great safety. That will beat inflation most years. Along the way, you also get some insurance coverage (see Chapter 8 for details).

2 BONDS. Most bonds expose you to more inflation risk, in return for more immediate income. There are government bonds, however, that do increase their interest rates with inflation. These might give you a consistent 3%–4% after inflation. This isn't much, but government bonds are very safe. Other bonds are less safe and more subject to inflation's ravages.

3 A "CHICKEN STOCK" PORTFOLIO. This is

In investing money, the amount of interest you want should depend on whether you want to eat well or sleep well.
—J. Kenfield Morley

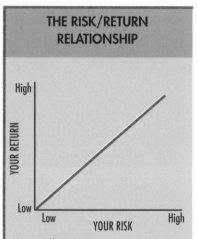

THE RISK/RETURN RELATIONSHIP

Low-risk investments pay a relatively low rate of return. You're not going to make a lot of money, but your risk of losing your investment is virtually nonexistent.

At the other end of the risk continuum, when there is the potential for great profit—and the potential for loss, usually this is "payment" for higher risk of loss.

Sounds good to me!

what I recommend for most people. It is designed for you to receive increased income every year, and increased asset value over time. This should beat inflation handily—and the returns for annuities and bonds—over longer periods of time, if the future is anything like the past.

4 A BASKET OF MORE AGGRESSIVE STOCKS WITH GREATER RISK AND GREATER POTENTIAL RETURN, SUCH AS UNIT TRUSTS COMPOSED OF TECHNOLOGY STOCKS. This is not recommended for those who want to minimize risk.

5 AGGRESSIVE STOCKS, SUCH AS INDIVIDUAL STOCKS WITH SPECIAL SITUATIONS. This could include trend following, turnarounds, timing situations, and other riskier approaches that I have not discussed in this book. This would usually be used with a small proportion of your assets. Not for the faint of heart.

Unfortunately, the latter two risky approaches are what most individual investors and stock advisors end up with, if they do not have the discipline of a system they believe in.

SAMPLE PORTFOLIOS

How should you start an investment program? My recommendations for you would depend on your answers to questions like those in Chapter 1 about your assets, needs, and your level of fear about the stock market. Even so, I won't use the fact that I don't know you as an excuse to avoid specifics here.

I do recommend that you find a financial advisor to help you. Unfortunately, as I mentioned in Chapter 9 (Hired Help), it will be fairly hard to find a superior advisor, and even harder to find one who will implement the concepts in this book. To make it easier to invest in Chicken Stocks, we are in the process of setting up unit trusts that would allow you to invest in my Chicken Stock portfolio without having a lot of money.

Now let's look at some "average" portfolios that my clients might use.

Portfolio #1
You Want Asset and Income Growth

Let's say that you have $500,000 in various retirement plans and investments and you don't need any extra income for a few years. In this case, if the market weren't going straight down at the time, I'd allot approximately 70% of your money to a Chicken Stock portfolio, spread among 15–25 stocks.

Depending on your interest in taking some risk for higher returns, I might put 30% of your money in higher-risk stocks such as technology or foreign stocks. I would follow the entire portfolio for you, so that you wouldn't have to worry about decisions.

Portfolio #2
Conservative: You Need Current Income

If you needed more income now than Chicken Stocks would provide, I might put you into a mix of regular bonds, convertible bonds, tax-free bonds, annuities, and

SAMPLE AVERAGE PORTFOLIOS

Portfolio #1
ASSET AND
INCOME GROWTH

30% Aggressive Stocks

70% Chicken Stocks

Portfolio #2
CONSERVATIVE: NEEDS CURRENT INCOME

40% Fixed Income Investments

60% Chicken Stocks

Portfolio #3
SUPER-CONSERVATIVE

50% Variable Annuity

50% Govt. Inflation-Indexed Laddered Bonds

Chicken Stocks. The proportions would depend on how much money you needed now and how much later. An average portfolio might contain 40% fixed income investments (laddered bond portfolio, for example) and 60% Chicken Stocks.

Portfolio #3 Super-Conservative

If you want to be absolutely conservative and protected against everything but the end of the world, I might put you in an annuity and government inflation-proof bonds (portfolio split about equally between the two). If you didn't have any retirement money accumulated, I would allot more to the annuity which allows larger contributions immediately.

And Now for the Standard Disclaimer...

Naturally, any of the above allotments of your assets would depend on the specifics of your situation. While this book can give you input to make your own decisions about investments, it is not the same as personal advice. The standard publishers' disclaimer on most advice books is correct: Books cannot substitute for personalized advice.

> Don't use "studying the situation" as an excuse to avoid a decision.

Since my approach to investing can last you for a lifetime, you don't have to rush into it. Take all the time you need and don't be swayed by whatever is happening in the market at the moment.

THE PSYCHOLOGY OF INVESTING

In investing, you can be your own worst enemy if you do not have a plan you are comfortable with and stick to it. Studies by academics show that investors have many judgment biases. For instance, behavioral finance researchers Daniel Kahneman and Mark Riepe discuss a series of biases that cause people to make mistakes in judgment.

Optimism

Kahneman and Riepe suggest that most people's beliefs are biased in the direction of optimism. Optimists exaggerate their abilities, and underestimate the likelihood of bad outcomes. Optimists are also prone to an illusion of control (that is, they exaggerate the degree to which they control their fate). They tend to underestimate the role of chance.

Hindsight

People can rarely reconstruct, after the fact, what they thought about the probability of an event before it occurred. Most are honestly deceived, as they exaggerate their earlier estimates of investment performance. In other words, people typically remember their successes and tend to forget about their mistakes.

False Causality

The tendency to attribute significance to chance fluctuations also leads investors to overreact to any information to which their attention is drawn. This same psychological quirk causes investors to perceive trends where none exist, and to take action on these erroneous impressions.

People Sell Winners, Not Losers

The price at which a stock was initially purchased determines whether selling a stock results in a gain or a loss.

An important consequence of this psychological fact is known as the *disposition effect:* a marked reluctance of investors to sell their losers. For example, consider an investor who needs cash and must sell one of two stocks that she owns; one of the stocks has gone up and the other has gone down.

"I know DotCom Corp. is at $2 and I bought it at $20. That's why I don't want to sell it. How far can a $2 stock fall, anyhow?"

In extensive studies of actual stock trading, Professor Odean at the University of California at Davis has shown that people tend to sell their winners and hold their losing stocks. This is the opposite of what you need to do for good investment returns. Unrealized gains are a great tax shelter. And stocks that have done well tend to continue to do well.

Few people are comfortable psychologically with selling losers. They prefer to wait until they might break even. By doing this, they end up holding their weakest stocks. If they'd sold the weaker stocks for a loss and put the money into stronger stocks, they would have had much better performance.

"Let your winners run and sell your losers" is the way to make profits in the stock market, not the other way around.

FAVORING THE "IN CROWD" (OF STOCKS)

Finance professor Robert Vishny (University of Chicago Business School) and others believe that investors underprice out-of-favor stocks while at the same time being irrationally overconfident about exciting growth companies. Not only do many investors foolishly like to follow the crowd, but they also get pleasure and pride from owning popular stocks.

Your Psychology

I could go on about the studies of the psychology of investing, but I won't. While there is some interesting material, it tends to be abstract and technical. You just need to think about your own "psychology" so you can achieve your goals.

WILL YOU OUTLIVE YOUR MONEY?

Your biggest concern should be whether or not you will outlive your money. Compounding the problem is the fact that inflation will continue to eat up the buying power of your life savings so that it will not

30-YEAR TREASURY BILLS: A DYING SPECIES

The US is the only major country in the world to offer 30-year Treasury bills. That comes from a time when inflation here was so bad that we needed the extra-long term to attract enough foreign investors. Now that we are the strongest country in the world, it's likely that the 30-year bonds will be largely phased out.

buy as much in the future as it does today.

With these facts in mind, it's imperative for you to create an investment portfolio that will produce higher income in the months and years ahead. In the long run, a fixed-income portfolio (bonds, certificates of deposit, T-bills) will fail to keep its value against rising prices. Its yield will not change, and the payback of principal will be in dollars that will not buy as much as the dollars that were originally invested. (The one exception to this rule is discussed in the bonds chapter.)

For example, the $6,260 annual income from a hypothetical 30-year $100,000 treasury bond bought in May 1976 would have seemed attractive at that time—6.26% is a good return. By maturity in 2006, however, that $6260 will be worth only about $1,725 in real 2006 dollars. The real value of the $100,000 will have shrunk to about $27,250. The principal may have been safe from market risk, but inflation risk devastated the value of the overall investment.

SUMMARY: WHAT WILL YOU DO NOW?

The real "psychological" and practical question is what will you do about your investing now. I've made some suggestions in this chapter that you can *you* have to take action to get results.

I know people who've left money in old IRAs getting minimum interest at the bank. I know people who've left major money in their checking accounts with low or no interest. Yet at the same bank, they could have bought a CD paying far more interest.

ACTION STEPS
1. Set a financial goal.
2. Get help as needed.
3. Invest.
4. Track your performance.
5. Make changes as necessary.
6. Repeat steps 1–5.

You bought this book because you wanted to take control of your investing. While it is a complicated area, I've shown you some simple things you can do by yourself, and some more complex things you can do with professional help.

Whatever you think will be best to improve your situation, I urge you to take action. Only through action do you receive accurate feedback. Only through action can you improve your situation. Only through action can you build your estate. Only through action can you ensure your financial future.

You can do it. This book shows you how to get started. It's up to you to begin.

I wish you good investing and many happy returns!

GLOSSARY

10-K. A detailed financial report that must be filed by a firm each year with the Securities and Exchange Commission. It is much more detailed than a typical annual report published and sent to shareholders.

12b-1 fees. An extra fee charged by some mutual funds to cover the costs of promotion and marketing. In practice, 12b-1 fees are often used to compensate brokers for selling low-load and no-load funds 401(k) plan. An employer-sponsored retirement plan that permits employees to divert part of their pay into the plan and avoid current taxes on that income. Money directed to the plan may be partially matched by the employer, and investment earnings within the plan accumulate tax-free until they are withdrawn. 403(b) plan. Similar to 401(k) plans, but set up for public employees and employees of nonprofit organizations.

Accrued interest. Interest that is due but hasn't yet been paid. It most often comes into play when you buy bonds in the secondary market. If you buy a bond halfway between interest payment dates, you must pay the seller for the three months' interest accrued but not yet received. You get the money back three months later when you receive the interest payment for the entire six-month period.

Alpha. A mathematical measure of price volatility that attempts to isolate the price movements of a stock from those of the market. A stock with a high alpha is expected to perform well regardless of what happens to the market as a whole. (See also Beta.)

American Depositary Receipt (ADR). US investors may buy shares in some foreign companies in the form of ADRs. The shares of the foreign corporation are held in the vault of a US bank and the holder is entitled to all dividends and capital gains.

The certificate, transfer, and settlement practices for ADRs are identical to those for US securities.

AMEX. American Stock Exchange.

Annual report. A corporate report detailing the preceding year's financial results and plans for the upcoming year.

Annuity. A series of regular payments, usually from an insurance company, guaranteed to continue for a specific time, usually the annuitant's lifetime, in exchange for a single payment or a series of payments to the company. With a deferred annuity, payments begin sometime in the future. A fixed annuity pays a fixed income stream for the life of the contract. With a variable annuity, the payments may change according to the investment success of assets in the policy.

Arbitrage. An attempt to profit from momentary price differences that can develop when a security or commodity is traded on two different exchanges.

Asset allocation. The process of dividing investment funds among different investment categories.

At-the-market. When you buy or sell a security "at-the-market," the broker will execute your trade at the next available price.

Back-end load. A fee charged by mutual funds to investors who sell their shares before owning them for a specified time.

Basis point. A measure used in quoting bond yields. One hundred basis points is equal to 1 percent. For example, if a bond's yield changes from 7.00 to 6.65 percent, it is a 35 basis-point move.

Bear market. A market in which prices of securities are falling or are expected to fall. Officially, a fall of at least 20% from the high.

Bearer bond. Also called a coupon bond, it is not registered in anyone's name. Rather, whoever holds the bond (the "bearer") is entitled to collect interest payments merely by cutting off and mailing in the attached coupons at the proper time. Bearer bonds are no longer being issued in the US.

Bearish. A bear thinks the market is going to go down. Bearish is the opposite of bullish.

Beta. In A stock a beta higher than 1 is expected to move up or down more than the market. A beta below 1 indicates a stock or fund that usually goes up and down less than the market. Often considered a measure of risk, but rarely a good one.

Bid/asked. On the stock market Bid is the price a buyer is willing to pay; asked is the price the seller will take. The difference, known as the spread, is the broker's share of the transaction.

Blue chip stocks. Stocks issued by large, well-established companies, widely held, often with good growth records and/or paying relatively stable dividends.

Boiler room. A high-pressure telephone sales operation, usually involving cold calls to people to sell risky investments.

Bond. An interest-bearing security (loan) that obligates the issuer to pay a specified amount of interest for a specified time, usually several years, and then repay the bondholder the face amount of the bond. Bonds issued by corporations are backed by corporate assets; in case of default, the bondholders have a legal claim on those assets Interest from corporate bonds is taxable; interest from municipal bonds, which are issued by state and local governments, is free of federal income taxes and, usually, income taxes of the issuing jurisdiction. Interest from Treasury bonds, issued by the federal government, is free of state and local income taxes but subject to federal taxes.

Bond rating. A judgment about the ability of the bond issuer to fulfill its obligation to pay interest and repay the principal when due. The best-known bond-rating companies are Standard & Poor's and Moody's. Their rating systems, although slightly different, both use a letter-grade system, with triple-A the highest rating and C or D the lowest.

Book value. The net-asset value of a company, determined by subtracting its liabilities from its assets and dividing the result by the number of shares of common stock. Not usually related to the actual stock value.

Broker. An individual registered to sell securities.

Bull market. A market that trends higher over a sustained, but undefined, period of time.

Bullish. A bull is someone who thinks the market is going to go up, which makes bullish the opposite of bearish.

Call feature. Allows the issuer to buy back a bond on specific date before maturity. These dates and prices are set when the bond is issued. Bonds are usually called when interest rates drop so significantly that the issuer can save money by issuing new bonds at lower rates.

Call Option. Stock option giving the holder the right to buy shares at a given price for a given period of time.

Capital gain distribution. A mutual fund's annual distribution to shareholders of the profits derived from the sale of stocks and bonds.

Capitalization. The value of a company as measured by the market price of its common shares, multiplied by the total number of shares that have been issued.

Certificate of deposit. Usually called a CD, a certificate of deposit is a short- to medium-term instrument (one month to five years) that is issued by a bank or savings and loan association to pay interest at a rate higher than that paid by a pass book account.

Chicken Stock. A stock with a consistent record (at least 12 years) of higher earnings every quarter and higher dividends every year. (See Chapter 3.)

Churning. Excessive buying and selling in a customer's account undertaken to generate commissions for the broker.

Closed-end investment company. Also called a closed-end fund. When the initial offering of shares is sold out, the closed-end fund trades on the stock market at a price determined by investor supply and demand.

Cold calling. The practice of brokers making unsolicited calls to people they don't know in an attempt to drum up business.

Commodities market. Exchanges that trade items like wheat, copper, sugar, and less "concrete" items as well such as foreign currencies. Very risky for individuals, as 90% of them lose money. Useful for the producers and users of commodities to lock in future prices. (See also *Futures trading*.)

Common stock. A share of ownership in a corporation.

Consumer Price Index (CPI). This index measures changes in prices paid by consumers for a variety of goods and services.

Contrarian. An investor who thinks and acts in opposition to the conventional wisdom.

Convertible bond. A bond that is exchangeable for a predetermined number of shares of common stock in the same company. Some preferred stock is also convertible to common stock.

Coupon. The part of a bond that evidences the amount of interest due and at what time and where the payment is to be made.

Crash. I define it as a 20% drop in a major market within two weeks or less. Used more generally as quick a breakdown in prices.

Currency hedging. A technique used to offset the risks associated with the changing value of any given currency using a commodity exchange.

Current yield. The annual rate of return on a security, calculated by dividing the interest or dividends paid by the current market price.

Cyclical industries or stocks. Industries where earnings tend to rise quickly when the economy strengthens and fall quickly when the economy weakens. Examples of cyclical industries include housing, automobiles, and paper.

Day trading. The speculative practice of both buying and selling the same stock or other investment in the same day. Trying to make money from short term fluctuations in prices.

Discount broker. A cut-rate firm that executes stock, bond and mutual fund orders but provides little in the way of research or other investment aids.

Discretionary account. A limited "power of attorney." A brokerage account in which the customer has given the broker the authority to buy and sell securities at his or her discretion, without checking with the customer first.

Diversification. Having money in different kinds of investments to attempt to increase safety.

Dividend. The share of company earnings paid out to stockholders.

Dividend reinvestment plan. Also called a DRIP, where a company automatically reinvests a shareholder's cash dividends in additional shares of common stock, often at no cost.

Dollar-cost averaging. Investing a set amount of money on a regular schedule regardless of the price of the shares at the time. In the long run, dollar-cost averaging tends to produce a lower average share cost because you buy more shares when the price is low.

Dow Jones Industrial Average. The oldest stock market average, which tracks the performance of 30 actively traded stocks of well-established, blue-chip companies and is designed to reflect the general US business scene.

Dow Jones Utility Average. A market indicator composed of 15 utilities stocks.

Dow Theory. A belief that a major trend in the stock must be confirmed by a new high or low in the Dow Jones industrial, transportation and utility averages.

Due diligence. The information gathering to investigate and understand an investment thoroughly before recommending it to a customer.

Ex-dividend. The period between the declaration of a dividend by a company or a mutual fund and the actual payment of the dividend. On the ex-dividend date, the price of the stock or fund will fall by the amount of the dividend, since new investors don't get the benefit of it. Companies and funds that have "gone ex-dividend" are marked by an X in the newspaper listings.

Expense ratio. A measure of the costs of running a mutual fund. The best tool for comparing the management costs you'll incur by investing in different funds.

Fannie Mae. The acronym for the Federal National Mortgage Association. It buys mortgages and sells off pieces to investors.

The Federal Reserve Federal (the Fed). The governing body of the Federal Reserve System, which is the central bank of the United States. Among other thins It adjusts the federal funds rate charged by one financial institution lending federal funds to another to affect the direction of interest rates.

Freddie Mac. The acronym for the Federal Home Loan Mortgage Corporation; it operates similarly to Fannie Mae.

Front-end load. The sales commission charged at the time of purchase of a mutual fund, insurance policy or other product.

Full-service broker. A brokerage firm that maintains a research department and other services .

Fundamentals. Characteristics of a company, such as revenue growth, earnings growth, financial strength, market share, and quality of management.

Futures trading. Trading in commodities that will be delivered at a future date.

Ginnie Mae. The acronym for the Government National Mortgage Association, which buys up mortgages and sells them to.

Gross domestic product (GDP). The total market value of all final goods and services produced in a country over a given period of time.

Growth investing. Investing in stocks which typically trade at higher prices relative to their earnings than value stocks, due to their higher expected earnings growth.

Hedging. Limiting your possible losses. For example, you might protect a stock against the risk of the market falling sharply by purchasing a corresponding put option which would increase in value as the stock price fell.

Individual Retirement Agreement (IRA). A tax-sheltered account that permits investment earnings to accumulate untaxed until they are withdrawn. There is an annual contribution limit, and penalties usually apply for withdrawals before age 59 1/2.

Inflation. A consistent rise in the general level of prices. Inflation is widely measured by the Consumer Price Index, an economic indicator that measures the change in the cost of purchased goods and services on the pocketbook level.

Initial public offering. A corporation's first public offering of an issue of stock. Also called an IPO.

Institutional investors. Mutual funds, banks, insurance companies, pension plans and others that buy and sell stocks and bonds in large volumes. Institutional investors account for 70% or more of market volume on an average day.

Junk bond. A high-risk, high-yield bond rated BB or lower by Standard & Poor's or Ba or lower by Moody's. Junk bonds tend to be issued by relatively unknown or financially weak companies, or they have only limited backing from reasonably solvent companies.

Keogh plan. A tax-sheltered retirement plan into which self-employed individuals can deposit up to 20% of earnings and deduct the contributions from current income.

Limit order. An order that specifies the highest or lowest price at which the customer is willing to trade securities. Margin buying. An investor can borrow from a brokerage firm up to half the purchase price of a stock or bond investment.

Maturity date. The date a bond expires, usually at face value.

Money-market funds. Mutual funds that invest in short-term debt. An ideal place to earn current market interest with a high degree of liquidity.

NASDAQ (pronounced Naz-dak). A stock market operated by The National Association of Securities Dealers. These stocks are traded by market makers with prices negotiated between them. Automated NASDAQ trades are done strictly by computer.

Net worth. The value of a company or individual after debts are subtracted.

No-load funds. Mutual funds that do not carry a sales commission.

Odd lot. A stock trade involving fewer than 100 shares. Since the smallest number of shares traded on a stock exchange is 100, an "odd lot" must be matched up with other "odd lots" in order to be traded on an exchange. Some brokerage companies will make an "odd lot" market for the convenience of their customers. For contrast, see *Round lot.*

Option. The right to buy or sell a security at a given price within a given time. The right to buy the security is called a "call." Calls are bought by investors who expect the price of the stock to rise. The right to sell a stock is called a "put. " Puts are purchased by investors who expect the price of the stock to fall. (See also *Warrant.*)

Over-the-counter market (OTC). A network of dealers who trade securities that are not listed on an exchange. There are almost 360,000 registered stock and bond representatives scattered across the country.

P/E ratio. The price-to-earnings ratio is calculated by dividing a stock's current price by its current earnings per share. A high number means that investors are optimistic about future growth and have bid up the stock's price.

Penny stock. Generally thought of as a recently issued stock selling for less than $5 a share and traded over the counter. They are considered high risk and most institutions will not buy them, limiting their market appeal.

Portfolio. A collection of securities owned by an individual or an institution that may include stocks, bonds, mutual funds, unit trusts, annuities and money market securities.

Preferred stock. A class of stock that pays a specified dividend set when it is issued. They appeal mainly to corporations, which get a tax break on their dividend income.

Prospectus. The document that describes a securities offering or the operations of a mutual fund, limited partnership or other investment. It must be given to every investor who purchases a new issue of registered securities.

Proxy. The formal authorization by a stockholder that permits someone else (usually company management) to vote in his or her place at shareholder meetings or on matters put to the shareholders for a vote at other times.

Put Option. Stock option giving the holder the right to sell shares at a given price. (See also *Call option.*)

Recession. A period of zero or negative economic growth and high unemployment. Technically, it must have negative growth for two quarters.

Return on equity. Obtained by dividing the total value of shareholders' equity—that is, the market value of common and preferred stock—into the company's net income after taxes.

Rollover. A tax-free transfer of funds from one tax-deferred retirement savings plan to another. If you take possession of the funds, the money must be deposited in the new account within 60 days. You can also use a rollover to transfer funds from a company plan—when you receive a lump-sum distribution, for example—to an IRA. The tax bill is delayed until you withdraw funds from the IRA.

Roth IRA. New in 1998, this is also known as a "back-loaded" IRA. Contributions are not deductible, but withdrawals can be completely tax-free in retirement.

Round lot. A hundred shares of stock, the smallest number of shares bought and sold on a stock exchange.

Sallie Mae. Acronym for the Student Loan Marketing Association, which buys student loans from colleges, universities and other lenders and packages them into units to be sold to investors.

Secondary market. The general name given to stock exchanges, the over-the-counter market and other marketplaces in which stocks, bonds, mortgages and other investments are sold after they have been issued and sold initially.

Sector. A group of securities that are similar with respect to industry, maturity, type, rating, or coupon.

Selling short. Selling an investment in the belief the price will fall and it may be bought at a lower price in the future. The investor borrows shares of a security from his or her broker and immediately sells them at the current price. Then, after the price of that security declines, an equal number of shares is bought on the open market to replace the borrowed shares. For instance, if you sell short 100 shares of XYZ Corp. at $70.00 a share and buy 100 shares back when the price drops to $40.00, your profit is $30 a share, or $3000. Short selling is not suitable for conservative investors because it involves unlimited risk. If you buy a share at $10, you can lose only $10. If you short sell a share at $10, you might have to replace it at $15, $20, $30, or more—there is no upper limit.

SEP IRA (Simplified Employee Pensions). As with Keogh plans, Designed as an easy-to-administer retirement plan, it can also be opened if you have self-employment income from a sideline business or free-lance work. Your contributions can be much higher than regular IRA plans allow.

Shorting. (See Selling short.)

Sinking fund. Financial reserves set aside to be used exclusively to redeem a bond or preferred stock issue.

Specialist. A member of the stock exchange who maintains an inventory of certain stocks and buys and sells shares as necessary to maintain an orderly market for those stocks.

Speculators. Investors who seek large capital gains through relatively risky investments.

Spread. The price difference between the highest bid and lowest ask for a security at a given point in time. It may also refer to an option-hedging strategy in which an investor has taken contrary positions in the same underlying stock simultaneously but with different strike prices or expiration dates.

Standard & Poor's 500 Index. A measure of stock prices based 500 widely held common stocks.

Stop-loss order. Instructions to a broker to sell a particular stock if its price ever dips to a specified level. It automatically converts to a market sell order when the predetermined level is touched. (See also *Limit order*.)

Street name. The description given to securities held in the name of a brokerage firm but belonging to the firm's customers. Holding stocks in street name facilitates trading because there is no need for the customer to pick up or deliver the certificates.

Technical analysis. An approach to market analysis that attempts to forecast price movements by examining and charting the patterns formed by past movements in prices, trading volume, the ratio of advancing to declining stocks and other statistics. For contrast, see *Fundamental analysis*.

Ticker tape. At one time, the price and volume of each stock trade was printed out on a narrow piece of paper as it occurred. Dedicated market watchers would "watch the tape" as it printed. Many electronic displays are designed to look somewhat like a "tape" of prices moving across the screen. The old tape was also thrown out the window for "ticker tape parades" down the street for heroes.

Treasury bills. Short-term debt issued by the federal government, sold at a discount and redeemed at full face value.

Treasury notes. Debt securities issued by the federal government that generally mature within 1 to 10 years.

Triple witching closeout. The third Friday of March, June, September, and December when options and futures contracts expire on market indices along with options on individual stocks. The simultaneous expirations often set off heavy buying and selling of options, futures and the underlying stocks themselves often creating large artificial moves in the stock market for the day.

Unit investment trust (UIT). A closed-end portfolio of securities sold in fractional, undivided interests (usually $1,000). (See Chapter 4.)

Warrant. An option to purchase shares of stock at a particular price for a specified period of time, but usually with a longer life than typical options. Often issued with new shares of stock and then traded separately.

Yield. The annual rate of return on an investment, expressed as a percentage.

Zero-coupon bond. A bond that pays all its interest at maturity but none prior to maturity. It may be redeemed at maturity for full face value. While it is bought at a discount.

ECONOMIC INDICATORS

Belge Book Report *(released by the Federal Reserve Board)*. Summary of regional economic conditions, prepared by the 12 Federal Reserve Banks for use at the central bank's next Federal Open Market Committee meeting.

Business Inventories *(released by the Commerce Department)*. Measure of the stocks of unsold goods held by US businesses.

Business Productivity and Costs *(released by the Labor Department)*. Measure of productivity—defined as output per number of hours worked—in the business and the nonfarm business sectors of the workplace.

Construction Spending *(released by the Commerce Department)*. Measure of construction spending on residential, nonresidential, and government projects.

Consumer Credit *(released by the Federal Reserve Board)*. Measure of money loaned to individuals, usually on an unsecured basis, requiring monthly repayment. Bank loans, credit cards, and installment credit are examples of consumer credit.

Consumer Price Index *(released by the Labor Department)*. Gauge of inflation that measures changes in the prices of consumer goods. The index is based on a list of specific goods and services purchased in urban areas.

Current Account *(released by the Commerce Department)*. The current account is the broadest measure of US trade with the rest of the world. It includes data not only about goods but also about merchandise and services, as well as some financial transactions.

Durable Goods Orders *(released by the Commerce Department)*. New orders for manufactured durable goods and shipments of durable goods. A durable good is a project that is expected to last more than three years.

Employment Cost Index *(released by the Labor Department)*. Changes in compensation costs, including wages, salaries, and employer costs for employee benefits.

Employment Situation *(released by the Labor Department)*. Tally of payrolls and the unemployment rate.

Existing Home Sales *(released by the National Association of Realtors)*. Regional report on home resale activity.

Factory Orders *(released by the Commerce Department)*. Tally of US manufacturers' shipments, inventories, and orders for consumer goods. Includes revised reports for durable goods.

Gross Domestic Product *(released by the Commerce Department)*. The total value of goods and services produced within the economy.

Housing Completions *(released by the Commerce Department)*. Survey of the number of privately-owned, completed single-and multi- family homes.

Housing Starts *(released by the Commerce Department)*. Monthly tally of the number of new privately-owned housing units started and housing permits issued by local government authorities.

Import and Export Price Indexes *(released by the Labor Department)*. Tally of price changes in US imports and exports.

Industrial Production and Capacity Utilization *(released by the Federal Reserve Board)*. Output at US factories, utilities, and mines. Capacity utilization is a measure of US industrial production as a percentage of total production capacity.

International Trade *(released by the Commerce Department)*. Tally of US international trade in goods and services, or the difference between a country's imports and exports.

Initial Jobless Claims *(released by the Labor Department)*. Number of Americans filing new claims for state unemployment insurance each week.

Leading Economic Indicators *(released by the Conference Board)*. Composite of 12 economic measurements developed to help forecast likely changes in the economy as a whole.

Merchandise Trade *(released by the Commerce Department)*. Measure of the US trade deficit or surplus in goods and services.

Monetary Aggregates *(released by the Federal Reserve Board)*. Weekly measures of money supply. M1 consists of funds that are readily available for spending, including cash and checking accounts. M2 consists of M1 and all savings or short-term deposits. It also includes certain short-term assets such as the amounts held in money-market mutual funds. M3 is the total of M1 and M2 as well as the assets and liabilities of banks.

National Association of Purchasing Management Index *(released by the National Association of Purchasing Management)*. Report on the pace of manufacturing activity in the US as a whole and in specific metropolitan areas. The report is based on data compiled from a survey of purchasing executives at more than 300 industrial companies.

New Homes Sales *(released by the Commerce Department)*. Sales of new single-family houses.

Personal Income and Outlays *(released by the Commerce Department)*. Tally of wage and salary disbursements and of personal consumption expenditures.

Philadelphia Federal Reserve Business Outlook Survey *(released by the Federal Reserve Bank of Philadelphia)*. Survey of regional business activity.

Producer Price Index *(released by the Labor Department)*. A group of statistics used to gauge inflation at the wholesale level. The index for finished goods, which tracks commodities that won't undergo further processing and are ready for sale to the ultimate user, is the most prominently reported of the statistics and is released monthly.

Real Earnings *(released by the Labor Department)*. Tally of real average weekly earnings of US workers. The data are collected from the payroll reports of private nonfarm establishments. Earnings of both full-time and part-time workers holding production or nonsupervisory jobs are included.

Retail Sales *(released by the Commerce Department)*. Sales of durable and nondurable goods to consumers.

Wholesale Trade Sales and Inventories *(released by the Commerce Department)*. Tally of the sales and inventories of US merchant wholesalers.

INDEX